Microsoft®
INTERNET
EXPLORER 3.0
Step by Step

Other titles in the *Step by Step* series:

For Microsoft Windows 95

Microsoft Access for Windows 95 Step by Step

Microsoft Access/Visual Basic for Windows 95 Step by Step

Microsoft Excel for Windows 95 Step by Step

Microsoft Excel/Visual Basic for Windows 95 Step by Step

Microsoft Exchange Step by Step

Microsoft Office 95 Integration Step by Step

Microsoft PowerPoint for Windows 95 Step by Step

Microsoft Project for Windows 95 Step by Step

Microsoft Visual Basic 4 Step by Step

Microsoft Windows 95 Step by Step

Microsoft Word for Windows 95 Step by Step

Microsoft Works for Windows 95 Step by Step

More Microsoft Windows 95 Step by Step

Upgrading to Microsoft Windows 95 Step by Step

For Microsoft Windows 3.1

Microsoft Access 2 for Windows Step by Step

Microsoft Excel 5 for Windows Step by Step

Microsoft Excel 5 Visual Basic for Applications Step by Step, for Windows

Microsoft Visual FoxPro 3 for Windows Step by Step

Microsoft Mail for Windows Step by Step, versions 3.0b and later

Microsoft Office for Windows Step by Step, version 4

Microsoft PowerPoint 4 for Windows Step by Step

Microsoft Project 4 for Windows Step by Step

Microsoft Word 6 for Windows Step by Step

Microsoft Works 3 for Windows Step by Step

Microsoft®
INTERNET
EXPLORER 3.0
Step by Step

Microsoft *Press*

PUBLISHED BY
Microsoft Press
A Division of Microsoft Corporation
One Microsoft Way
Redmond, Washington 98052-6399

Library of Congress Cataloging-in-Publication Data
Microsoft Internet explorer 3.0 step by step / Catapult, Inc.
     p.   cm.
   Includes index.
   ISBN 1-57231-300-5
    1. Microsoft Internet Explorer.   2. Internet (Computer network)
3. World Wide Web (information retrieval system) 4. Microsoft
Network (Online service) I. Catapult, Inc.
TK5105.875.I57M53 1996
005.7'1369--dc20   96-9010
                                   CIP

Printed and bound in the United States of America.

1 2 3 4 5 6 7 8 9 RM–T 1 0 9 8 7 6

Distributed to the book trade in Canada by Macmillan of Canada, a division of Canada
Publishing Corporation.

A CIP catalogue record for this book is available from the British Library.

Microsoft Press books are available through booksellers and distributors worldwide. For further
information about international editions, contact your local Microsoft Corporation office. Or
contact Microsoft Press International directly at fax (206) 936-7329.

Apple and Macintosh Week are registered trademarks of Apple Computer, Inc. AltaVista
is a trademark of Digital Equipment Corporation. Microsoft, Microsoft Press, MS, MS-DOS,
Windows, and Windows NT are registered trademarks and ActiveMovie, ActiveX,
Authenticode, FrontPage, MSN, and NetMeeting are trademarks of Microsoft Corporation.

Other product and company names mentioned herein may be the trademarks of their
respective owners.

Companies, names, and/or data used in screens and sample output are fictitious unless
otherwise noted.

For Catapult, Inc.
Managing Editor: Diana Stiles
Writers: Patricia J. Atherly;
   Katherine M. MacDonald
Project Editor: Annette Hall
Technical Editors: Karen A. Deinhard;
   Vincent J. Abella
Indexer: Julie Kawabata

For Microsoft Press
Acquisitions Editor: Casey D. Doyle
Project Editor: Laura Sackerman

Catapult, Inc. & Microsoft Press

Microsoft Internet Explorer 3.0 Step by Step has been created by the professional trainers and writers at Catapult, Inc., to the exacting standards you've come to expect from Microsoft Press. Together, we are pleased to present this self-paced training guide, which you can use individually or as part of a class.

Catapult, Inc., is a software training company with years of experience in PC and Macintosh instruction. Catapult's exclusive Performance-Based Training system is available in Catapult training centers across North America and at customer sites. Based on the principles of adult learning, Performance-Based Training ensures that students leave the classroom with confidence and the ability to apply skills to real-world scenarios. *Microsoft Internet Explorer 3.0 Step by Step* incorporates Catapult's training expertise to ensure that you'll receive the maximum return on your training time. You'll focus on the skills that can increase your productivity the most while working at your own pace and convenience.

Microsoft Press is the book publishing division of Microsoft Corporation. The leading publisher of information about Microsoft products and services, Microsoft Press is dedicated to providing the highest quality computer books and multimedia training and reference tools that make using Microsoft software easier, more enjoyable, and more productive.

Table of Contents

Table of Contents

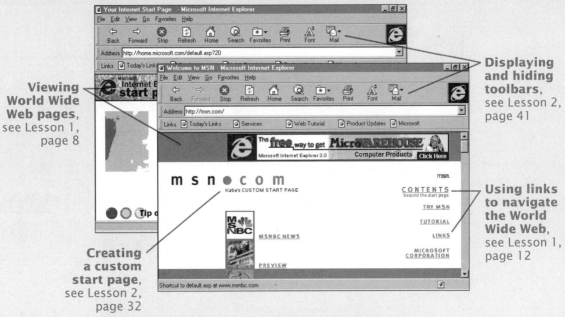

Viewing World Wide Web pages, see Lesson 1, page 8

Displaying and hiding toolbars, see Lesson 2, page 41

Using links to navigate the World Wide Web, see Lesson 1, page 12

Creating a custom start page, see Lesson 2, page 32

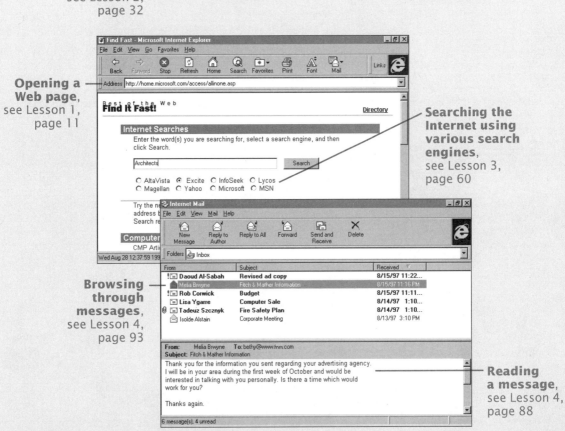

Opening a Web page, see Lesson 1, page 11

Searching the Internet using various search engines, see Lesson 3, page 60

Browsing through messages, see Lesson 4, page 93

Reading a message, see Lesson 4, page 88

*Quick*Look Guide

Posting a new article, see Lesson 5, page 119

Responding to the author of a message, see Lesson 4, page 90

Replying to a message, see Lesson 4, page 89

Displaying newsgroups, see Lesson 5, page 106

Subscribing to newsgroups, see Lesson 5, page 108

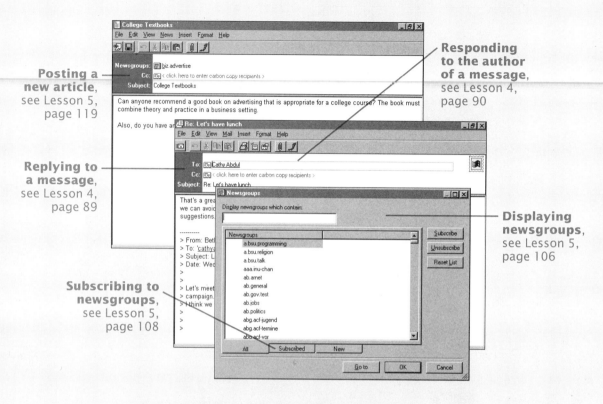

Using the Whiteboard drawing tools, see Lesson 6, page 135

Using the Whiteboard in NetMeeting to illustrate ideas, see Lesson 6, page 134

Viewing related articles and responses, see Lesson 5, page 112

Reading an article, see Lesson 5, page 111

Using the Whiteboard color palette, see Lesson 6, page 135

Accepting a call from a NetMeeting user, see Lesson 6, page 129

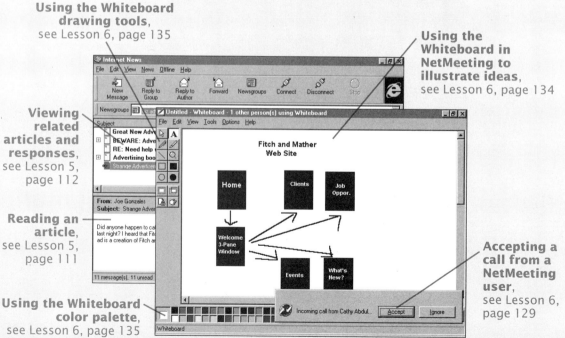

Finding Your Best Starting Point

Microsoft Internet Explorer 3.0 is a powerful Web browser program. With this book, you'll quickly and easily learn how to use Microsoft Internet Explorer 3.0 to explore the Internet and much more.

 IMPORTANT This book is designed for use with Microsoft Internet Explorer 3.0 for the Windows 95 and Windows NT version 4.0 operating systems. To find out what software you're running, you can check the product package or you can start the software, click the Help menu at the top of the screen, and click About Microsoft Internet Explorer. (If you need some help starting the software, see Appendix A, "Setting Up Your Internet Connection" and Appendix B, "Setting Up Internet Mail, Internet News, and NetMeeting.") If your software is not compatible with this book, a Step by Step book for your software is probably available. Many of the Step by Step titles are listed on the second page of this book. If the book you want isn't listed, please visit our World Wide Web site at http://www.microsoft.com/mspress/ or call 1-800-MSPRESS for more information.

Finding Your Best Starting Point in This Book

This book is designed for readers learning Microsoft Internet Explorer for the first time and for more experienced readers who want to learn and use the new features in Microsoft Internet Explorer 3.0. Use the following table to find your best starting point in this book.

If you are	Follow these steps
New... to computers to graphical (as opposed to text-only) computer programs to Windows 95 or Windows NT	**1** Become acquainted with your operating system and how to use the online Help system by working through the material "If You Are New to Windows 95 or Windows NT," which can be found on the accompanying CD-ROM in the file Newtowin.htm. **2** Learn basic skills for using Internet Explorer by working sequentially through Lessons 1 through 3. Then, you can do Lessons 4 through 6 in any order. To learn how to use e-mail, do Lesson 4. To learn how to use newsgroups, do Lesson 5. To learn how to use NetMeeting, do Lesson 6.

If you are	Follow this step
Switching... from Netscape Navigator from WinCim from Mosaic from NetSurfer	➤ Learn basic skills for using Microsoft Internet Explorer by working sequentially through Lessons 1 through 3. Then, you can work through Lessons 4 through 6 in any order.

If you are	Follow these steps
Upgrading... from Internet Explorer 2.0 or earlier	**1** Learn about the new features in this version of the program that are covered in this book by reading through the following section, "New Features in Internet Explorer 3.0." **2** Complete the lessons that cover the topics you need. You can use the table of contents and the *Quick*Look Guide to locate information about general topics. You can use the index to find information about specific topics.

If you are	Follow these steps
Referencing... this book after working through the lessons	**1** Use the index to locate information about specific topics, and use the table of contents and the *Quick*Look Guide to locate information about general topics.
	2 Read the Lesson Summary at the end of each lesson for a brief review of the major tasks in the lesson.

New Features in Internet Explorer 3.0

The following table lists the major new features in Microsoft Internet Explorer 3.0 that are covered in this book. The table shows the lesson in which you can learn how to use each feature. You can also use the index to find specific information about a feature or a task you want to do.

To learn how to	See
Create a Custom Start Page.	Lesson 2
Have Internet Explorer warn you when you are transmitting personal information to an unsecure site or downloading information from a site.	Lesson 2
Restrict access to Web sites containing material you find objectionable.	Lesson 3
Use the Mail button to communicate with other people on the Internet using the fully integrated Internet Mail and Internet News programs.	Lesson 4 (e-mail) and Lesson 5 (newsgroups)
Conduct meetings over the Internet using NetMeeting.	Lesson 6

Corrections, Comments, and Help

Every effort has been made to ensure the accuracy of this book and the contents of the accompanying CD-ROM. Microsoft Press provides corrections and additional content for its books through the World Wide Web at

http://www.microsoft.com/mspress/support/

If you have comments, questions, or ideas regarding this book or the accompanying CD-ROM, please send them to us.

Send e-mail to

mspinput@microsoft.com

Or send postal mail to

Microsoft Press

Attn: Step by Step Series Editor

One Microsoft Way

Redmond, WA 98052-6399

Please note that support for the Internet Explorer 3.0 software product itself is not offered through the above addresses. For help using Internet Explorer 3.0, you can call Microsoft Internet Explorer AnswerPoint at (206) 635-7123 on weekdays between 6 a.m. and 6 p.m. Pacific time.

Visit Our World Wide Web Site

We invite you to visit the Microsoft Press Word Wide Web site. You can visit us at the following location:

http://www.microsoft.com/mspress/

You'll find descriptions for all of our books, information about ordering titles, notice of special features and events, additional content for Microsoft Press books, and much more.

You can also find out the latest in software developments and news from Microsoft Corporation by visiting the following World Wide Web site:

http://www.microsoft.com/

We look forward to your visit on the Web!

Using the Microsoft Internet Explorer 3.0 Step by Step CD-ROM

The CD-ROM inside the back cover of this book contains practice files that you'll use as you do the exercises in the book. For example, when you're learning how to use the Whiteboard in Microsoft NetMeeting, you'll open one of the practice files—a .wht file of a Whiteboard diagram. By using the practice files, you won't waste time creating the samples used in the lessons—instead, you can concentrate on learning how to use Internet Explorer, Internet Mail, Internet News, and NetMeeting. By using the practice files and the step-by-step instructions in the lessons, you'll also learn by doing, which is an easy and effective way to learn and remember new skills.

 IMPORTANT Before you break the seal on the practice CD-ROM package, be sure that this book matches your version of the software. This book is designed for use with Microsoft Internet Explorer 3.0 for the Windows 95 or the Windows NT version 4.0 operating system. To find out what software you're running, you can check the product package or you can start Internet Explorer, click the Help menu at the top of the screen, and click About Internet Explorer. If your software is not compatible with this book, a Step by Step book for your software is probably available. Many of the Step by Step titles are listed on the second page of this book. If the book you want isn't listed, please visit our World Wide Web site at http://www.microsoft.com/mspress/ or call 1-800-MSPRESS for more information.

When you look at the Microsoft Internet Explorer 3.0 Step by Step CD-ROM, you will find several things on it:

- Internet Explorer 3.0 Starter Kit
- A copy of the Web site used in Lesson 1 and Lesson 2
- Internet shortcuts to all the Web Picks mentioned in the book
- A file with a list of glossary terms
- A file with a list of the practice files
- A file with the list of Web Picks and their abbreviated names
- A file with basic information and illustrations about how to use Windows 95 and Windows NT.

Install the practice files on your computer

Follow these steps to install the practice files on your computer's hard disk so that you can use them with the exercises in this book.

 NOTE If you are new to Windows 95 or Windows NT, you might want to work through "If You Are New to Windows 95 or Windows NT," which is on the accompanying CD-ROM in the file Newtowin.htm before you install the practice files. To open the appendix, insert the CD-ROM and double-click the file.

1 If your computer isn't already on, turn it on now. If you are using Windows 95, you might see a dialog box asking for your username and password. If you are using Windows NT, press CTRL+ALT+DEL to display the log on dialog box. Type the requested information in the appropriate boxes, and then click OK. If you see the Welcome dialog box, click the Close button.

If you do not know your username or password, contact your system administrator for help.

2 Remove the CD-ROM from the package inside the back cover of this book, and then insert the CD-ROM in your CD-ROM drive.

3 On the taskbar at the bottom of your screen, click the Start button, and then click Run.

The Run dialog box appears.

4 In the Open box, type **d:setup** (if the CD-ROM drive is drive D). Don't add spaces as you type.

5 Click OK, and then follow the directions on the screen.

The setup program window appears with recommended options preselected for you. For best results in using the practice files with this book, accept these preselected settings.

6 When the files have been installed, remove the disc from your CD-ROM drive and replace it in the package inside the back cover of the book.

A folder called Internet Explorer 3.0 SBS Practice has been created on your hard disk, and the practice files have been put in that folder.

Microsoft
Press
Welcome

NOTE In addition to installing the practice files, the Setup program created a shortcut on your Desktop to the Microsoft Press World Wide Web site. You can double-click the shortcut to visit the Microsoft Press Web site. You can also connect to the Web site directly at http://www.microsoft.com/mspress/

Using the Practice Files

Each lesson in this book explains when and how to use any practice files for that lesson. When it's time to use a practice file, the book will list instructions for how to open the file. The lessons are built around scenarios that simulate a real work environment, so you can easily apply the skills you learn to your own work. For the scenarios in this book, imagine that you work at Fitch & Mather, an advertising agency, and have been given the new account of Awesome Computers' Amazing Mouse.

The screen illustrations in this book might look different from what you see on your computer, depending on how your computer has been set up. Because the Internet is such a dynamic environment, you might have to improvise for some of the steps. To reduce inconsistencies, a Web site has been specially designed as a companion to this book. The Web site will not change, so you should be able to learn the skills taught with little variance from the steps.

For those of you who like to know all the details, here's a list of the material included on the practice disc:

Name	Description
Aweinfo.doc	A Microsoft Word document that you can use to practice sending files to other participants of a NetMeeting conference.
Awesome.wht	A graphic file that you and your practice partner can edit using the NetMeeting Whiteboard.
Stats.doc	A Microsoft Word document that you can use to share and collaborate with a partner.
Setup	The Internet Explorer 3.0 Starter Kit. Full installation includes Internet Mail, Internet News, ActiveMovie, HTML Layout Control, and Macromedia Shockwave.

The Microsoft Netmeeting program is located in the Internet Explorer Starter Kit in the Internet Explorer 3.0 folder.

Name	Description
Fitch & Mather Web site	An example of a corporate Web site for the fictional company Fitch & Mather.
Web Picks	Internet shortcuts.
Glossary.htm	Definitions of the important terms used in this book.
Newtowin.htm	An introduction to the basics of the Windows 95 and Windows NT operating systems, the mouse, and the Help system.

Need Help with the Practice Files?

Every effort has been made to ensure the accuracy of this book and the contents of the CD-ROM. If you do run into a problem, Microsoft Press provides corrections for its books through the World Wide Web at:

http://www.microsoft.com/mspress/support/

We also invite you to visit our main Web page at:

http://www.microsoft.com/mspress/

You'll find descriptions for all of our books, information about ordering titles, notices of special features and events, additional content for Microsoft Press books, and much more.

Conventions Used in This Book

You can save time when you use this book by understanding, before you start the lessons, how instructions, keys to press, and so on are shown in the book. Please take a moment to read the following list, which also points out helpful features of the book that you might want to use.

 NOTE If you are unfamiliar with Windows 95, Windows NT, or mouse terminology, see "If You Are New to Windows 95 or Windows NT," which is on the accompanying CD-ROM in the file Newtowin.htm.

Conventions

- Hands-on exercises for you to follow are given in numbered lists of steps (1, 2, and so on). An arrowhead bullet (➤) indicates an exercise that has only one step.
- Text that you are to type appears in **bold**.
- A plus sign (+) between two key names means that you must press those keys at the same time. For example, "Press ALT+TAB" means that you hold down the ALT key while you press TAB.

■ The following icons identify the different types of supplementary material:

	Notes labeled	Alert you to
	Note or Tip	Additional information or alternative methods for a step.
	Important	Essential information that you should check before continuing with the lesson.
	Troubleshooting	Possible error messages or computer difficulties and their solutions.
	Web Pick	Information about interesting World Wide Web sites.

Other Features of This Book

■ You can learn about options or techniques that build on what you learned in a lesson by trying the optional "One Step Further" exercise at the end of each lesson.

■ You can get a quick reminder of how to do the tasks you learned by reading the Lesson Summary at the end of a lesson.

■ You can quickly determine what online Help topics are available for additional information by referring to the Help topics listed at the end of each lesson. The Help system provides a complete online reference to Internet Explorer, Internet Mail, Internet News, and NetMeeting.

■ You can practice the major skills presented in the lessons by working through the Review & Practice sections at the end of each part. These sections offer challenges that reinforce what you have learned and demonstrate new ways you can apply your new skills.

■ You can learn how to use Microsoft Exchange in Lesson 4, "Using E-mail," by reading the shaded boxes that appear throughout the lesson.

■ You can use the Glossary provided on the Microsoft Internet Explorer 3.0 Step by Step CD-ROM to look up definitions of any terms that are unfamiliar to you. Double-click the glossary.htm file to open the glossary.

■ You can use the World Wide Web page shortcuts that are located on the Microsoft Internet Explorer 3.0 Step by Step CD-ROM to visit the Web site. Double-click the Web Pick to have Internet Explorer open that site.

■ You can practice the major skills presented in Lesson 1 and Lesson 2 by working offline with the Fitch & Mather fictional Web site provided on the Microsoft Internet Explorer 3.0 Step by Step CD-ROM. Double-click the Default.htm file to open the fictional Web site.

Learning to Browse the World Wide Web

Traveling the World Wide Web

Estimated time
30 min.

In this lesson you will learn how to:

- Start Internet Explorer.
- Move around in the Internet Explorer window.
- Travel the World Wide Web.
- Save a Web page and a Web graphic to your hard disk.

The Internet is one of the hottest technological topics in the news today. The Internet is a virtually limitless source of information about both professional and personal interests. On the Internet, you can research a term paper, evaluate a product you are thinking of purchasing, get up-to-the-minute stock market information, and communicate with anyone in the world, without ever leaving your chair. Leaders in the computer industry are proclaiming the World Wide Web (also called the Web or WWW) as the wave of the future for both businesses and individuals, so it is not surprising that interest in the Web increases daily. Your choice of Microsoft Internet Explorer as your Internet program will make your introduction to the information superhighway an easy and enjoyable journey.

WEB PICK   Get a glimpse of some of the coolest Web sites on the Internet today by visiting the Project Cool Web page at http:// www.projectcool.com

---

The Internet and the Web: What's the Difference?

The terms *Internet* and *World Wide Web* are considered to be interchangeable by some people, but the World Wide Web is actually the newest part of the Internet. The Internet is a worldwide network of computers that store information. The World Wide Web part of the Internet contains information presented in the form of Web pages, which can contain text, graphics, video, and sound, unlike the older, text-only parts of the Internet. In text-based parts of the Internet, you need to use special commands and must either know where to find the information you want or use text-search programs to find it. Web pages can also contain links to each other so that you can move from one page to related pages simply by clicking a link. The Web is fun and easy to use, which has made it the fastest growing part of the Internet.

Using Internet Explorer to Travel the Web

World Wide Web information is organized in sections called *Web pages*, and the location where related Web pages are stored is called a *Web site*. The Web site is the equivalent of a house, and the Web pages are the rooms of the house. And just like a house, a Web site can be made up of a wide range of rooms (from only a few to hundreds, even thousands). The World Wide Web is made up of hundreds of thousands of Web sites on hundreds of thousands of computers. You can, for example, begin your search of the Web at the London Stock Exchange Web site, and within seconds you can be looking at the tourist spots in Ishikawa, Japan. A few seconds later, you can be at the Louvre Web site. Looking at a Web site thousands of miles away is as easy as opening a document on your hard disk.

Who Created the Internet?

Once upon a time, the Internet was owned by the government, more specifically, by the Department of Defense's Advanced Research Project Agency (ARPA). The man who developed this early Internet was Bob Taylor, director of computer research at ARPA. His goal was to find a way for people using different types of computers, such as Apple computers, PCs, and UNIX-based computers, to share data with each other. This "baby" Internet connected military bases, universities, and companies working for the government to each other. Eventually, the number of people using the Internet grew to the point where the government became concerned about security; so the Internet was split in half. Half, named MILNET, was reserved for the military. The other half, which evolved into the Internet of today, was reserved for education. Eventually, by popular demand, the Internet was made public.

The problem with having so much information freely available is that you can get lost on the Internet faster than you can in a strange town! Originally, to have access to the Internet, a user had to type in a long string of command codes. Any error, even something as minor as a misplaced comma, could change your destination or completely block your access to the Internet. But as the Internet has matured, the tools to view it have become easier to use.

How Do Computers "Talk" to Each Other?

When you travel around the Internet, or the "Net," your computer searches for information at exactly the same time as thousands of other computers are searching for information. With hundreds of thousands of computers around the world speaking to each other practically simultaneously, how can they all understand each other? Well, not only can computers "talk" and "listen" at the same time, they all use the same language when they communicate. This "language," which is not a language but a common method of communication, is called *TCP/IP*. (TCP/IP, if you are curious, stands for Transmission Control Protocol/Internet Protocol.) TCP/IP uses a complex set of rules that guide communications between all computers.

Web pages are files created in a formatting language called *hypertext markup language* (HTML). At one time you needed to know all the coding symbols, or *tags*, of HTML to design a Web page. Naturally, Web page creation was limited to those experts who spoke "computerese." Now, Web-page programs, such as Microsoft FrontPage, have automated the process of Web page design.

What's an Intranet?

It is common for companies to distribute and share information with the people within their organization. By using an intranet, a company can have a central location for documents it wants to share with its workers. An *intranet* is a private group of interconnected computers—such as a company-wide network—that stores information in much the same manner as the Internet. Information that needs to be shared and distributed in a company, such as an employee handbook, the sales results for last quarter, or any important company news, can be placed on the company's intranet. It can be presented in the same format that would be used to place it on the World Wide Web. The information in an intranet is usually protected by a password or other security measures to ensure that only authorized users can view the pages. You move around an intranet the same way you move around on the Internet: by clicking links, typing URLs, and using a browser such as Internet Explorer. An intranet can reduce the cost of distributing information, and can make it more timely.

Your computer must translate the HTML symbols of a Web page before you can view the Web page on your computer. A program called a *browser* translates the HTML tags into a Web page you can view on your monitor. Browsers have made the Internet accessible to everyone, not just programmers or other computer experts. Internet Explorer is a powerful browser that can help you "surf" the Internet.

Starting Microsoft Internet Explorer

Before you can use Internet Explorer, you have to connect to the Internet. The two most common ways of doing this are through a *network connection*, which directly connects computers together, or through a dial-up connection. A *dial-up connection* is a "middle-man" that uses a piece of communication hardware, called a modem, to send messages and files between computers over telephone lines. If you have a network connection, you can open Internet Explorer and connect automatically to the Internet. If you use a dial-up connection, you must first use your modem to connect to your Internet service provider, such as The Microsoft Network (MSN), before you can use Internet Explorer.

 NOTE For more information about how to set up a dial-up connection, see Appendix A, "Setting Up Your Internet Connection." For more information about network connections, contact your system administrator.

In your work at Fitch & Mather, an advertising company, you research materials for advertising campaigns. You have heard that the Internet is a great data-collection tool. The Internet supposedly has a lot of freely available information, and you want to explore tools that might make your job easier and help you be more efficient. You have mentioned this to your manager, and she wants you to research the Internet for possible long-term use by the company. You have selected The Microsoft Network as your Internet service provider, and now you're ready to begin exploring the Internet.

 NOTE If you haven't set up The Microsoft Network, see Appendix A, "Setting Up Your Internet Connection."

Start Internet Explorer

In this exercise, you connect to The Microsoft Network, and then start Internet Explorer so you can start exploring the World Wide Web.

IMPORTANT To successfully complete this lesson, you will need to have a computer, a modem, and a dial-up connection to an Internet service provider, or a connection to the Internet through a network. In addition, you must have Internet Explorer 3.0 installed. See Appendix A, "Setting Up Your Internet Connection," for more information.

Some service providers charge hourly rates for their services. If you are using one of these providers, you might want to read through the lesson before starting the exercises. This will minimize the amount of time you spend connected to your service provider.

The Internet

If you are connected to the Internet through a network connection, skip steps 2 through 4.

If you have forgotten your password, you can call the MSN Member Support Center at 1-800-386-5550.

Modem icon

1 On the Desktop, double-click The Internet icon.

The Internet Explorer window opens, and if you have selected MSN as your service provider, The Microsoft Network Sign In dialog box appears. If you have not installed The Microsoft Network, a dialog box appears asking if you want to install it.

2 In the Member ID box, type your Member ID.

This is the name you gave yourself when you set up The Microsoft Network.

3 In the Password box, type your password.

If you don't want to type your password every time you connect to The Microsoft Network, select the Remember My Password check box. But remember, if you choose this option, anyone using MSN on your computer has access to your MSN account.

4 Click Connect.

The Microsoft Network Sign In dialog box closes. After a few moments, the Microsoft Internet Explorer Start Page opens. If you are using a modem, you will see a small modem icon in the status box, on the right side of the taskbar.

 TROUBLESHOOTING If you can't connect to The Microsoft Network, try the following: check your modem settings, verify that your modem is turned on (if it is an external modem) and connected to a phone jack, and then check that you are using the correct phone number. If you still cannot connect, contact your Internet service provider or see your system administrator.

Maximize

5 On the upper-right corner of the Internet Explorer window, click the Maximize button.

The Internet Explorer window expands to fill the entire screen. Your screen should look similar to the following illustration.

Toolbar—
Address— box

Viewing Pages on the World Wide Web

When you use Internet Explorer to view Web pages on the World Wide Web, you "browse" these Web pages. Web pages are identified by their Uniform Resource Locator, or URL. The *URL* is the unique location of a Web page, much like your street address is your unique mailing address in the world. The URL is composed of four parts: the service type, the host name, the directory path, and the filename. You don't need to know what the parts mean to use the Web, but it is easier to understand where a Web page is if you understand the basic syntax of URLs, at least a little bit. The address http://www.microsoft.com/ie/default.htm is an example of a URL; and the following table describes each of a URL's components.

Component	Meaning	Description
http://	Service type	http stands for Hypertext Transport Protocol. Your browser uses the service type of the address to determine how to display the information from a Web page on your screen.
www.msn.com	Host name	Web site that stores the Web pages on a Web server.
/ie/	Directory path	Path to the Web page.
default.htm *or* default.html	Filename	Filename of the Web page.

What Are the Service Types?

In your use of Internet Explorer, you might come across service types other than http. The following table describes the different service types you might encounter.

Service type	What it gives access to
file://	A file on your hard disk or a floppy disk. You can save a copy of a Web page on your computer. When you open the copy, its URL changes to the location where it was saved on your hard disk. Saving Web pages to your hard disk will be discussed later in this lesson.
ftp://	A location that contains large data files that you copy to or from your computer. FTP stands for File Transfer Protocol, which is a special way to send and retrieve files over the Internet.
gopher://	A menu-based index of information available on the Internet.
http://	http stands for Hypertext Transfer Protocol, which is a special coding system for Web pages.
telnet://	A protocol that allows you to use your keyboard to control a computer at another location.
wais://	A software search program that contains indexes of information available on the Internet; Wais is similar to Gopher.

 NOTE Some Web pages have the filename extension html, instead of the filename extension htm. Htm files were created on personal computers, which most often use filename extensions that are three characters long. Html files were created on computers that can have filename extensions that are more than three characters long. There is no other difference between the two file types.

Web pages can change daily or a Web site can be removed from the Web at any time. Because the Web is a dynamic place, sometimes when you go to a Web site you will receive an error message. When you get an error message, it means either that Web site is temporarily not available or that it no longer exists. Try opening the site later or, if the information is duplicated somewhere else on the Web, try another site.

Browsing Web Pages

Now that you are connected to the Internet, you can view any page on the Web that is accessible to the public. But, before you can move from page to page, you need to know how.

When you first open Internet Explorer, you are greeted by the Microsoft Internet Explorer Start Page. This page acts as a starting place for your Web search. The Microsoft Internet Explorer Start Page is a Web page, supplied by Microsoft, that contains links and tools that help you move around the Web more easily. A *link*—sometimes known as a hotlink, a hyperlink, or a jump—is a picture or group of words that, when clicked, automatically connects your computer to the selected page or text. You can tell whether a picture or a group of words is a link by looking at its formatting: a picture jump is typically surrounded by a colored border, and a text jump is underlined or in color. Another way to tell whether a picture or a group of words is a link is to position your mouse pointer over the area. If the mouse pointer changes to a pointing hand, you are over a link. You can create a custom Start Page that contains links to your favorite sites. You will learn more about customizing your Start Page in Lesson 2, "Personalizing Your Web Environment."

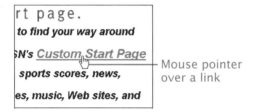

Mouse pointer over a link

From the Start Page, you can view other pages on the Web by either typing a URL in the Address box or clicking a link. If you know the exact address of the Web site you want to connect to, it's probably easiest to type in the site's URL. Otherwise, you can navigate from page to page by clicking the links that interest you.

NOTE Text links are starting to be replaced by graphical images composed of hotspots. *Hotspots* are areas of a graphic that have been linked to Web pages. Hotspots work similarly to text links, but are harder to identify. If you think a graphic might be a jump to another page, place your mouse pointer over it. If the mouse pointer changes to a pointing hand, then the graphic is a link.

Internet Hosts and Host Names

A *host* is typically the company or organization that contains the computer that holds the Web site that you view on the Internet. Several different types of companies and organizations can have sites on the Internet, and each has a unique name. The last three letters of a host name tell you what type of organization runs the Web site. The following table gives some examples of host name abbreviations and describes the type of organization associated with each abbreviation.

Type	Description
com	A commercial site, such as a corporation.
edu	An educational site, such as a university.
gov	A government site.
mil	A military site.
net	A network site.
org	A miscellaneous organization site.

You are ready to start exploring the Internet. As you are about to begin, your manager stops by and tells you that she'd like you to start your exploration of the Web by visiting your company's Web site. In the following exercises, you view the Microsoft Internet Explorer Start Page, type an Internet address to move to the Fitch & Mather's Web site, and use links to travel the Web.

Examine the Microsoft Internet Explorer Start Page

1   Take a look at the information on the Microsoft Internet Explorer Start Page.

    The title bar shows you the title of the current Web page; in this case, the page title is Your Internet Start Page. The page is separated into different sections, called *frames.* Each frame shows a different Web page of the Web site. Frames make it possible to view different Web pages on one Web page.

 NOTE   The URL for the page and the title of the page are two separate items. The URL is the Internet address of the page; the title of the page is what the page has been named by its creator.

---

2   In the Address box, locate the URL.

    The Address box is just below the toolbar. The URL for the Microsoft Internet Explorer Start Page is http://home.microsoft.com/. The "com" indicates that the Microsoft Internet Explorer Start Page is a commercial host.

You can also click Open on the File menu.

The http:// service type is automatically inserted at the beginning of the URL.

3 Click in the Address box.

The URL located in the Address box should be highlighted. If not, drag to select the entire URL.

4 In the Address box, type **www.microsoft.com/mspress/fnm** and then press ENTER.

The home page for the Fitch & Mather Web site opens. The *home page* is the introductory page of a Web site. The Start Page that opens when you start Internet Explorer is the home page for the Microsoft Web site. It is given the special name of Start Page, because you can start here and jump to other Web pages. Your screen should look like the following illustration.

Fitch & Mather logo

IMPORTANT   The path and filename in a URL are case-sensitive, which means that the word "Computer" is not the same as the word "computer." Be sure to type a URL exactly as it is shown, or you will receive an error message when you try to open the Web page.

Use links and hotspots to explore the Web

In the following exercise, you explore the Fitch & Mather Web site.

1 Position the pointer over the Fitch & Mather logo.

The pointer changes to a pointing finger, which indicates that this graphic is a hotspot.

2 Click the Fitch & Mather logo.

The Fitch & Mather menu page opens.

3 In the left frame, click the Our Clients button.

This button is also a hotspot. A list of clients appears in the bottom-right pane.

4 In the left frame, click the Useful Links button.

The Fitch & Mather Internet Useful Links Web page replaces the list of clients in the bottom-right pane.

5 Click the Advertising Age link.

The Advertising Age home page opens. This Web page doesn't appear in the bottom-right pane because you have jumped to another Web site.

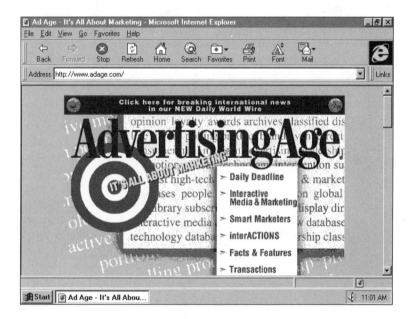

 WEB PICK   Keep current on the United States' attempts to boldly go where no one has gone before by visiting the NASA home page at http://www.nasa.gov

Returning to Web Sites

As you search the Web, you will find Web sites that you want to revisit. While you surf the net, Internet Explorer keeps a record of the URLs of the Web pages that you visit. Internet Explorer keeps this record in two places: on a brief address list and in a more complete History folder. You can also revisit Web sites by using toolbar buttons.

The Address box contains a drop-down list that holds the URLs of up to twenty-six Web sites. If you visit more than twenty-six Web sites, the one that has been on the list the longest is removed, and the new one is added.

The URLs of various Web sites are also stored in the History folder. The History folder stores Internet shortcuts to all of the Web sites you have visited during a set number of days. The default number of days is 20, but you can change it to as few as zero days, in which case none of the URLs of the sites you visit will be stored, or to as many as 999 days. These addresses take up space, so keep your hard disk size in mind when you define the length of time you want to save addresses. Using the History folder, you can return to any page you have viewed within the designated number of days, regardless of the amount of time between visits.

Internet shortcuts contain pointers to the URL of a Web page regardless of where that page is located on the Internet. When you go to a Web page, Internet Explorer automatically creates an Internet shortcut to that page, and to every other Web page that you visit. When you double-click an Internet shortcut, or select a URL from a menu, the corresponding Web page opens, just as clicking a link opens another Web page.

Another way you can revisit Web pages, during the same session, is to use the Back, Forward, and Home buttons on the toolbar to move between pages you have recently viewed, or to return to your Start Page. If you quit Internet Explorer, and then start the program again, you can't use the Back button and the Forward button to view Web pages you visited in an earlier session; the buttons will be usable only after you visit some pages during the current session. On the other hand, the Home button will always function, even at the start of a session. The following table describes the Back, Forward, and Home buttons.

Button	Description
	Move back through the Web pages you have visited during the current session, one page at a time. The Back button is not available when you are viewing the first Web page you opened in a session.
	Move forward through Web pages you have visited during the current session, one page at a time. The Forward button is not available when you are viewing the last Web page you opened in a session.
	Move to your Start Page. The Home button is always available.

Revisit a Web site

In the following exercises, you revisit Web sites by using the Address list and the History folder.

1 Click the Address down arrow, and then click http://www.microsoft.com/mspress/fnm/.

The Fitch & Mather home page opens.

NOTE Only the URLs of Web sites that you have previously typed in the Address box appear in this list. Web sites that you have used links or hotspots to visit are not listed.

2 On the Go menu, click Open History Folder.

The contents of the History folder are displayed in the Internet Explorer window. All the URLs of the Web pages you have visited in the past 20 days are listed.

3 Double-click the Our Clients Internet shortcut icon.

The Our Clients Web page opens. The page doesn't contain any frames.

Use the Back button and the Forward button

You can also click Back on the Go menu.

1 On the toolbar, click the Back button.

The Fitch & Mather home page opens.

2 Click the Back button again.

The Advertising Age home page opens.

3 On the toolbar, click the Forward button.

The Fitch & Mather home page opens.

You can also click Forward on the Go menu.

4 Click the Forward button again.

The Fitch & Mather Our Clients page opens.

WEB PICK Visit the SportsLine Web page for lots of sports goodies, at http://www.sportsline.com

Return to the Microsoft Internet Explorer Start Page

➤ On the toolbar, click the Home button.

The Microsoft Internet Explorer Start Page opens.

NOTE If you use a link on a Web page to move to a different Web page, and then return to the original page, the link you used will typically appear in a different color than before you clicked it. The change in color indicates that you have already used this link. This is a way of knowing whether you have visited a Web page before. If the Web page has been changed to include new information before you revisit it, Internet Explorer will restore the link to its original color.

Controlling Web Page Viewing

The first time you open a Web page, it takes some time for the page to appear, or to load, on your computer. But, when you use the Forward button and the Back button, the pages load much faster. This is because they do not have to be downloaded from the Web site. Instead, they are stored in a folder that Internet Explorer uses to temporarily hold graphics and Web pages on your computer. The Internet Files folder stores a copy of the text, the graphics, and any other files associated with the Web page. By default, the storage capacity of the folder is limited to 3 percent of your available hard disk space. When the folder is full, files are automatically deleted, starting from the oldest Web page viewed, until new Web page files can be added.

 NOTE You can empty the folder by clicking Options on the View menu. Then, click the Advanced tab, click Settings, and click Empty Folder. Click Yes. Click OK twice.

Every time you open a Web page, it is retrieved from the Internet and added to the Internet Files folder. When you return to a page during a session, if Internet Explorer finds a copy of the page in the folder, then Internet Explorer loads the Web page from the contents of the folder, not from the Web site where the page is located. Since Internet Explorer does not have to download the page from the Web site, the page appears much faster.

 TIP Some Web pages, such as those that have news or stock information, have time-sensitive information and change many times a day. In that case, you can ask Internet Explorer to check if the Web pages have changed every time you view them. Here's how: Choose Options from the View menu. Click the Advanced tab. Under Temporary Internet Files, click Settings. Click the Every Visit To The Page option. Click OK.

If you return to a site that you visited earlier, and that site is unavailable, Internet Explorer might use the copy of the Web page that's stored in the Internet Files folder. If you are not sure that the information you are viewing is current, use the Refresh button, which tells Internet Explorer to reload the Web page. You can also use the Refresh button to reload a page that did not get completely copied to your computer, for whatever reason. Typically, you will be warned of a potential problem by an error message.

If you find that, while loading a Web page that contains a large graphic, the time required is much too long, you can stop the loading process by clicking the Stop button.

Why Can't I Get Access to a Web Site?

There are a couple reasons why you might not be able to view a Web site. Each Web site is stored on a computer, so, if the computer is not on, you won't be able to gain access to the site. Also, each site contains a connection to the Internet, similar to the connection you make to the Internet. These connections can handle only a certain number of people trying to view the same information simultaneously. The number of people a site can handle depends on the size of its connection. If a site is glutted by requests for access, and you try to gain access to it, you will get an error message. If you get a message informing you that the site is unavailable, try connecting again later. Internet service providers also have the option of blocking access to certain Web sites or newsgroups.

Reload the Web page

In this exercise, you reload a page and stop a page from loading.

1 On the toolbar, click the Refresh button.

   The Microsoft Internet Explorer Start Page reloads.

2 Click the Back button.

   The Fitch & Mather Our Clients page opens.

3 Click the Refresh button.

   The Fitch & Mather Our Clients page reloads.

Cancel the opening of a Web page

In this exercise, you cancel the Web page opening.

1 Click the Home button.

   The Microsoft Internet Explorer Start Page opens.

2   Click the Refresh button.

The reloading of your Start page begins.

3   Click the Stop button.

The reloading stops.

Saving a Web Page for Easy Access

During your journeys on the Internet, you will find Web pages that you want to view again and again. You could search your History folder for the Web pages you want to view; but after a while, there will be so many pages referenced in the History folder that the search for the right page will become more difficult. That's why Internet Explorer offers a Favorites folder in which you can store the addresses of your favorite pages. When you add a Web page to your Favorites folder, Internet Explorer creates an shortcut to that page.

Add a Web page to your Favorites folder

You want to explore the Web more, and want to start by opening the Census Web site. Since you know that you will want to visit this site regularly, you want to find a way to connect to it easily in the future without having to go through the Fitch & Mather Internet site. In this exercise, you add the Census Web site to your Favorites folder.

1   Click the Address down arrow, and then select
http://www.microsoft.com/mspress/fnm/

The Fitch & Mather Internet home page opens.

2   Click the Fitch & Mather logo.

The Fitch & Mather menu page opens.

3   In the left frame, click the Useful Links button.

The Useful Links page opens.

4   Click the Census link.

The US Census Bureau home page opens.

5   On the toolbar, click the Favorites button.

A menu opens.

6   Click Add To Favorites.

The Add To Favorites dialog box appears.

NOTE To create a folder in which to organize your Web pages, click the Create In button, click the New Folder button, type a name for the folder in the Folder Name box, and then click OK. Verify that the folder you created is selected. It will appear as an open folder if it is.

7 Click OK.

The US Census Bureau home page has been added to your Favorites folder. The Add To Favorites dialog box closes.

 8 On the toolbar, click the Home button.

The Microsoft Internet Explorer Start Page opens.

9 Click the Favorites button, and then click the US Census Bureau Home Page.

The Census Web page opens.

 WEB PICK Visit a Web site that contains all the lyrics of the popular informational cartoons of School House Rock, at http://iquest.com/~bamafan/shr

Saving Web Pages and Graphics

When you travel the Web, you will come across certain Web pages that contain information or graphics that you want to save for later reference. Using Internet Explorer, you can save a specific Web page or graphic to your hard disk. Saving a Web page is similar to adding an Internet shortcut to your Favorites folder, but instead of saving a file that contains the URL to take you to the Web page at the Web site, this file contains the contents of the Web page at the time you saved it, and will not change.

Web pages are pieced together from different types of files, such as text files, graphics files, and multimedia files. When you save a Web page to your computer, you cannot save the entire page as one file. You have to save each file that comprises the Web page separately. For example, you have to perform different save operations if you want to save the text, the graphics, and the multimedia files of one Web page. It doesn't matter which type of file you save first, but if you want to re-create the Web page on your computer, you should save all the files that were used to construct the original Web page.

You can save Web pages as HTML files or as text files. The following table summarizes the advantages and disadvantages of saving a Web page as an HTML file and as a text file.

> **Do I Have to Wait for My File to Download Before I Can Move to Another Web Site?**
>
> No. Typically when you leave a Web page, your connection with that page is broken, and a connection is made to the new Web page or Web site. In Internet Explorer, however, you can open a special downloading dialog box. You tell Internet Explorer whether you want to open a file or save it to your computer, and then the File Download dialog box stays open until the selected action is completed. While this is going on, you can switch to the Internet Explorer window and view a different Web page without breaking the connection between your computer and the site from which you are downloading. You can even download more than one file at a time. But, remember, every additional task you perform slows the speed of your download because your computer is doing more and more things at the same time.

Type of file	Advantages	Disadvantages
HTML	Looks the same as it did on the Web when you use Internet Explorer to view it. Contains all the HTML codes used to create the page.	Difficult to understand when displayed in programs such as Microsoft Word for Windows. HTML tags are visible, but not their results.
Text	Easy to copy text from the Web page into a word-processing document or Notepad.	Contains no HTML tags, so the file cannot be opened as a Web page in Internet Explorer.

HTML code

```
home_microsoft(1).htm - Notepad
File  Edit  Search  Help
<HTML>
<HEAD>
 <TITLE>
  Your Internet Start Page
 </TITLE>
<META http-equiv="PICS-Label" content='(PICS-1.0 "http://www.rsac.org/ratings'

</HEAD>
<FRAMESET ROWS="53,*" FRAMEBORDER=0 FRAMESPACING=0>
    <FRAME SRC="/above.asp?169"
    NAME="Above" SCROLLING=no>
    <FRAME SRC="/welcome.asp" NAME="lower">
</FRAMESET>
<NOFRAMES>
<CENTER>
This site is specially designed for users of Microsoft Internet
Explorer 3.0.
```

Save a Web page on your computer

You have been asked by your manager to save the home page of the Fitch & Mather Web site so that it can be sent to a sister company to duplicate. In this exercise, you will save the home page from the Fitch & Mather Web site, including the HTML codes, to your hard disk.

1 Click the Address down arrow, and then select http://www.microsoft.com/mspress/fnm/.

2 On the File menu, click Save As File.

The Save As dialog box appears.

3 Click the Save In down arrow, and click Desktop.

The Desktop is a good place to save files if you are not sure where you will eventually want to store them. You can move them just as you would any other file after they are saved to your hard disk.

4 In the File Name box, type **Fitch & Mather**

5 Be sure that HTML (*.htm, *.html) appears in the Save As Type box, and then click Save.

 NOTE If you want to save the page as a text file, click the Save As Type down arrow, and then select Plain Text (*.txt).

Copying Files from a Web Page to Your Computer

The Web is a great source of information. Some of this information is in the form of files that you can copy, or *download,* to your computer. For example, if you want to check out a new computer game, you can go to Web sites that have copies of the game demo that you can download to your computer. Downloadable files can be software programs, text files, spreadsheets, graphics, or multimedia files. Many of the files you find will be in the public domain; these files are called *freeware*. Another kind of software file available on the Net is called *shareware*. You don't pay for shareware when you download it. When you start the program, however, the address of the vendor and the price of the program are usually on the first screen.

Compressing/ decompressing utilities are available as shareware or can be purchased at your local computer software store.

Files available for copying from the Internet are usually *compressed*. Compressed files have been squeezed together so that they occupy less space. These files are usually identified by extensions such as ZIP or EXE. Compressed files cannot be used until they are *decompressed,* or returned to their original size. Some compressed files are *self-extracting*, which means they decompress themselves when you click them. If you download a compressed file that is not self-extracting, you need to decompress it by using a program such as PKUnzip. See

Lesson 4, "Using E-mail," for more information about compressing and decompressing files.

When the file is finished copying, the Windows Software Security dialog box opens. This box will appear every time you save an executable file that has not been signed by its creator. If a file is signed by its publisher, then the file is guaranteed not to have viruses. See Lesson 2, "Personalizing Your Web Environment," for more information about security.

IMPORTANT Damaging programs known as *viruses* might infect programs you download from the Internet. Viruses range from irritating to incapacitating. To protect your computer and your files from serious damage, you should buy an anti-virus program. These programs protect your computer from the most common viruses, but anti-virus programs are not 100 percent foolproof, so use caution when downloading programs or files from the Internet.

Download a file to your computer

The Manager of New Accounts has placed a file on the Fitch & Mather Products page to celebrate the new Awesome Computer account. This file is called Neko. In this exercise, you will copy the Neko file to your computer.

1   Click the Fitch & Mather logo.

    The Fitch & Mather menu page opens. Be sure that the Our Clients page is in the bottom right frame. If it isn't, click the Our Clients button.

2   In the Our Clients window, scroll down, and then click the Neko link.

    The File Download message appears. After a few moments, an Internet Explorer dialog box appears.

3   Be sure that the Save It To Disk option is selected, and then click OK.

    The Internet Explorer dialog box closes, and the Save As dialog box appears.

You can also double-click the My Computer icon and double-click Drive C.

4   Click the Save In down arrow, scroll down, and click My Computer.

    My Computer opens.

5   In the Folder View box, click Drive C, and then click Open.

    You will save the file in a new folder on Drive C.

6   Click the Create New Folder button, type **Neko** and then press ENTER.

    A new folder named Neko is created.

Create New Folder

7   Select the Neko folder, click Open, and then click Save.

The File Download message appears. The estimated time that the download will take appears at the bottom of the box. The size of a file and the speed of your modem determine how long this process will take. The larger the file and the slower the modem, the longer the download. Some files can take hours to download if they are large. This one is small, so it should take only a few minutes regardless of the speed of your modem.

 TIP   You can save a file anywhere you want to, but it is easiest to save it on the Desktop and then move it to the folder where you want to save it permanently.

Open the file

You have decided that you want to see what this Neko file is right away, so you decide to install it to your hard disk. In the following exercise, you open the file.

1   Minimize the Internet Explorer window.

2   Double-click My Computer, double-click Drive C, and then double-click the Neko folder.

The Neko folder opens.

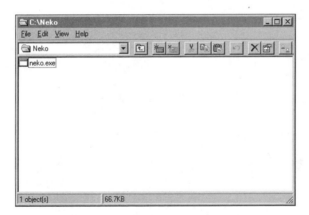

3   Double-click the Neko icon.

An MS-DOS window opens, and the contents of the Neko compressed file are expanded into the Neko folder.

If you have
Windows NT,
the MS-DOS
window closes
automatically.

4 On the MS-DOS Finished window, click the Close button.

The DOS window closes.

5 In the Neko window, double-click the Neko95 icon and then move your mouse pointer to a blank area on the Desktop.

The Neko program starts. Neko, a small graphic of a cat, appears on your Desktop and will follow your pointer.

6 Double-click the Neko95 icon.

The program closes, and Neko disappears from the Desktop.

7 Close all open windows.

8 On the taskbar, click the Internet Explorer button.

The Internet Explorer window is maximized.

Saving an Internet Graphic File

*To save graph-
ics and Web
pages without
opening them,
use the right
mouse button
to click the
item you want,
and then click
Save Target As
on the shortcut
menu.*

As you explore the Web, you will see thousands of graphics files displayed on thousands of Web pages. Some of these graphics might be in the *public domain*, which means the graphic or file is free to the public. If a graphic is in the public domain, typically that information will be noted. If there is no mention of the graphic's copyright status, you shouldn't copy it. It is against the law to use a graphic or file without the permission of its owner. You can, however, save graphics and files that are in the public domain and use them in your own documents. Using the menu, you can use the Save Picture As command, or you can drag the graphic from a Web page to the appropriate folder. If the document to which you want to save the graphic is open, you can drag the graphic from the Internet Explorer window directly to the document.

How Do I Work with Internet Graphics?

Two types of graphics file formats are used on the Internet: GIF (Graphics Interchange Format) files and JPEG (Joint Photographic Experts Group) files. Both of these file types are *bitmaps*. Bitmaps are graphic images composed of small dots, or *bits*. Using Internet Explorer, you can save these GIF or JPEG files in their original format, or you can save them in a generic format called Bitmap. You can tell if a graphics file is in the bitmap file format, because the filename extension is BMP. An advantage of saving a graphic as a BMP file is that you can also recolor, modify, and resize the graphic if you have a program for that graphics format. The disadvantage of saving a graphic as a BMP file is that a Bitmap is often very large, and it can take up a lot of space on your hard disk.

Save a graphic

You are giving an in-depth presentation on the progress of the ad campaign to the President of Awesome Computers, and you want to include the Fitch & Mather Web page logo in your presentation materials. In this exercise, you save the graphic file to your computer.

 IMPORTANT When you use the Save Picture As command to save a graphic, you must let the graphic load onto your computer before you can save it to your hard disk.

1 In the left frame, click the Home link.

The Fitch & Mather home page opens.

2 Use the right mouse button to click the Fitch & Mather logo.

A shortcut menu opens.

3 Click Save Picture As.

The Save As dialog box appears.

 NOTE You should save the graphics file as a GIF or JPEG if you want to re-create the Web page using Internet Explorer. If you want to manipulate the graphics file, you might have to save the graphic as a BMP, depending upon the capabilities of your graphics application.

4 Verify that the graphic is being saved to your Desktop as Fitch & Mather, and then click Save.

You can also drag the graphic to your Desktop.

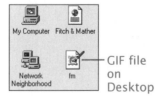

Viewing a Saved Web Page

You can view saved HTML files by using Internet Explorer and view text files by using a text editor program such as Notepad. If you double-click an HTML file located on your computer, it opens in Internet Explorer. If you double-click a plain text file, the file opens in Notepad. To see the HTML tags in the file, you can open the HTML file in Notepad. You do not have to be connected to the Internet, or online, to view either of these files saved on your computer.

 TIP . You don't have to save a file to view HTML tags. In Internet Explorer, you can quickly view the HTML tags of a Web page while online. On the View menu, click Source. Notepad automatically opens, and the HTML tags appear in the Notepad window.

View a Web page saved on your computer

You want to make sure that you saved the Web page properly, so you want to open the file you saved to your computer in Internet Explorer to confirm this. In this exercise, you open the Fitch & Mather home page file.

Minimize

You can also click Open on the File menu, and then click Browse.

1   On the Internet Explorer window, click the Minimize button.

    The Internet Explorer window is minimized.

2   On the Desktop, double-click the Fitch & Mather icon.

    The Internet Explorer window is maximized, and the Fitch & Mather home page appears as shown in the following illustration. Notice that the Address box lists the page URL as C:\WINDOWS\DESKTOP\Fitch & Mather.htm.

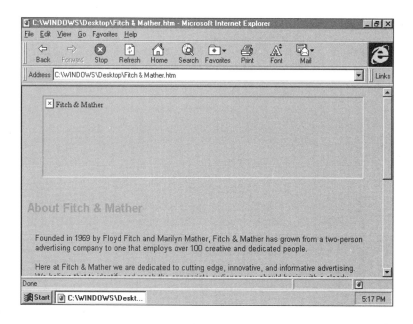

Printing Web Pages

If you want to share information on a Web page with someone who does not have Internet access, you can print it. When you print a Web page, the text and any graphics on the page are printed. The quality of the printout depends on the quality of your printer.

 TIP   If you want to print every link and the URL of the Web page that corresponds to each link, select the Print Shortcuts In A Table At The End Of The Document check box at the bottom of the Print dialog box. If you select this option, a table of all the links and the URLs of their corresponding Web pages is printed after the Web page prints.

Print a Web page

One of your co-workers who does not have Internet access has asked you to print out the Our Clients page from the Fitch & Mather Web site for her. In this exercise, you print a Web page.

 IMPORTANT   Your computer must be connected to a printer in order for you to complete this exercise. If your computer is not connected to a printer, skip to the end of the lesson.

1   Click the Address down arrow, and then select http://www.microsoft.com/mspress/fnm/.

The Fitch & Mather home page opens.

2   Click the Fitch & Mather logo.

The Fitch & Mather menu page opens.

3   In the left frame, click the Our Clients button.

The Our Clients page opens in the Internet Explorer window.

4   Click in the frame that contains the Our Clients Web page.

When printing a Web page that has frames, you must select the frame you want to print.

5   Click the Print button.

The Print dialog box appears.

6   Click OK.

The Our Clients Web page prints.

NOTE If you'd like to build on the skills that you learned in this lesson, you can do the One Step Further. Otherwise, skip to "Finish the lesson."

One Step Further: Saving Web Pages Without Opening Them

If you're in a hurry, you can quickly save a link to a Web page without going to the Web page itself. You can do this by saving an Internet shortcut, like the ones created in your Favorites folder.

During your experimentation on the Internet, you have found that you frequently refer to the Advertising Age link on the Fitch & Mather Useful Links page. In this exercise, you save an Internet shortcut to the Advertising Age Home page so that you can quickly open the Advertising Age Home page.

1 In the left frame of the Fitch & Mather menu page, click the Useful Links button.

   The Useful Links page opens in the Internet Explorer window.

Restore

2 On the Internet Explorer window, click the Restore button. Resize the window as necessary to view the Desktop.

   The Internet Explorer window is reduced.

3 Drag the Advertising Age link to your Desktop.

   An Advertising Age shortcut icon appears on your Desktop. Be sure to hold down the mouse button when you drag the link to the Desktop. Otherwise, you will jump to the Advertising Age page.

Finish the lesson

1 To continue to the next lesson, click the Home button.

2 If you are finished using Internet Explorer for now, on the File menu, click Close.

   The Microsoft Network dialog box appears. If you are not using a dial-up service provider, skip step 3.

3 Click Yes.

   Your modem is disconnected, and Internet Explorer closes.

4 Delete any items on your Desktop created during this lesson, and close all open windows.

Lesson Summary

To	Do this	Button
Connect to The Microsoft Network	Double-click The Microsoft Network icon. Enter your Member ID and your password, and then click Connect.	
Start Internet Explorer	Double-click The Internet icon. Connect to your service provider, if necessary.	
View your Custom Start Page	Click the Home button.	Home
Use links	Click a link.	
Open a Web page	Type the Web page URL in the Address box.	
Revisit a Web site	Click the Address down arrow, and then click the site you want.	
Reload a Web page	Click the Refresh button.	Refresh
Download a file	Click the link of the file to download the file. Click the Save It To Disk option, and then click OK. Select the location you want the file copied to, and then click Save. Click Yes.	
Cancel the opening of a Web page	Click the Stop button.	Stop
Add a Web page to your Favorites folder	On the Favorites menu, click Add To Favorites. Click the Add button.	
View a favorite Web page	Click the Favorites button, and then double-click a Web page name.	Favorites
Save a Web page on your computer	On the File menu, click Save As File. Choose a location to store the file, and then click Save.	
Save a graphic	Use the right mouse button to click the graphic. Click Save Picture As. Choose a location to store the file, and then click Save.	
View a saved Web page	Double-click the Web page icon.	Print
Print a Web page	Click the Print button.	

For online information about	On the Help menu, click Help Topics. In the Help Topics dialog box, click Index, and then type
Viewing The Microsoft Start Page	**start page**, and then display Returning to
Opening a Web page	**Web pages**, and then display Viewing by clicking hyperlinks *or* Viewing by using addresses
Revisiting a Web site	**History folder**, opening
Reloading a Web page	**Web pages**, and then display Speeding up the display of
Canceling the opening of a Web page	**Stop button**
Adding a Web page to your Favorites folder	**Favorite pages**, and then display Collecting
Saving a Web page	**saving**, and then display Pages as files on your computer
Saving a graphic	**pictures**, and then display Saving on your computer

Personalizing Your Web Environment

In this lesson you will learn how to:

Estimated time
30 min.

- Create your Custom Start Page.
- Change your Start Page to another Web page.
- Reorganize your toolbar.
- Hide multimedia files to view Web sites faster.
- Change the fonts and colors of visited and unvisited links.
- Customize your History folder.
- Set a Web graphic as Desktop wallpaper.

When you're in your own home, you probably feel comfortable. All your possessions are around you and they're all in just the right place. You usually know where to find things, and you can get to them anytime you need to use them. Your Microsoft Internet Explorer is your home on the Web and, just like you've organized your home, you'll probably want to put everything in just the right place in the program window. In Internet Explorer, you can move toolbars around or hide them entirely. You can change Web link colors and text colors to suit your preferences. In addition, when you want to get information quickly, you can optimize the time you spend browsing by opening a site without opening its video, sound, and picture files.

Lesson 1 discussed opening and browsing Web pages, saving Web pages to your Favorites folder, and printing Web pages; but to make use of all that, you need to know what sites are available to you. Each day more sites appear on the

Web, but how do you know which sites are worth visiting and where to find them? Using a personalized Custom Start Page on The Microsoft Network, you can learn about Web sites and organize the Web site addresses that you visit most often. You can use your Custom Start Page as an organizing tool and as a launching point onto the Web.

In this lesson, you'll personalize your Internet Explorer window by creating a Custom Start Page. Then, you'll make Internet Explorer a little more comfortable, just like a home, by customizing it.

Creating a Custom Start Page

When you open Internet Explorer, the Microsoft Internet Explorer Start Page automatically opens in your window. You don't have to type a Web address or press a key; the page simply opens. However, in the Microsoft Internet Explorer Start Page, you can create your own Custom Start Page. Your Custom Start Page is really your launch point onto the World Wide Web. You can change your default settings so that your Custom Start Page opens in the Internet Explorer window every time you start the program or click the Home button.

When you open the Custom Start Page for the first time, it is pretty generic. It contains links to Microsoft sites and to some Web sites that are new or interesting to a general audience. You can leave the page as it is, but why do that? Internet Explorer gives you the option of personalizing your Custom Start Page so that it displays the information and links that interest you. You can also make your Custom Start Page more meaningful to you by adding links to the cool sites that you find on the Web and display information about topics such as news, movies, music, sports, and the weather. For example, if you frequently visit the CNET Web site, you can save the link to the CNET home page on your Start Page. Then, when you want to go directly to the CNET home page from your Start Page, you can simply click the link.

Setting Up Your Custom Start Page

As an employee of Fitch & Mather, you have installed Internet Explorer on your computer and are familiar with the basics of surfing the Net. You want to create your Custom Start Page so that you can use it as a tool to help you with your research, and you can have some fun too. You also want to be able to easily open Web pages that you frequently visit, and stay up to date on new and interesting Web sites.

To begin personalizing your Custom Start Page, you need to display it and give The Microsoft Network some information; then you can select links, news, and—yes—fun stuff to add to your page. When you finish personalizing your Custom Start Page, the links that you added will appear in the Internet Explorer window.

> ### What's in a Connection?
>
> The speed at which your modem can transfer information helps to determine the speed at which you will be able to move around on the Internet. The faster the modem, the more satisfying your Internet experience will be. Modems are separated into categories based on bits per second (bps). The higher the bps number, the faster your connection to the Internet will be, and the faster Web graphics and text will appear. To make your Internet experience a success, you should have, as an absolute minimum, a 14,400-bps (sometimes written 14.4 K bps) modem.

Start Internet Explorer

 IMPORTANT   To successfully complete this lesson, you will need to have a computer, a modem, and a dial-up connection to an Internet service provider or a connection to the Internet through a network. In addition, you must have Internet Explorer 3.0 installed.

1   On the Desktop, double-click The Internet icon.

The Internet Explorer window opens, and the Microsoft Network Sign In dialog box appears. If you have not installed The Microsoft Network, a dialog box appears asking if you want to install it.

2   In the Member ID box, type your Member ID.

This is the name you gave yourself when you set up The Microsoft Network.

3   In the Password box, type your password.

If you don't want to type your password every time you connect to The Microsoft Network, click the Remember My Password check box. Use caution if you choose this option, because then anyone using MSN on your computer has access your MSN account.

4   Click Connect.

After a few moments, The Microsoft Network window and the MSN Today window open. If you are using a modem, on the taskbar, you will see a small Modem icon in the status box.

 TROUBLESHOOTING   If you cannot connect to The Microsoft Network, try the following: check your modem settings, verify that your modem is turned on (if it is an external modem) and connected to a phone jack, and check that you are using the correct phone number.

5   Maximize the Internet Explorer window.

The Internet Explorer window expands to fill the entire screen.

 WEB PICK   Visit the High Five site to find out what's hot (and what's not) on the Web. This site critiques Web pages for design, conception, execution, and content. A new critique is posted every Wednesday. Find High Five at http://www.highfive.com/

Telling The Microsoft Network Your Personal Preferences

To personalize your Custom Start Page, you need to display The Microsoft Custom Start Page in the Internet Explorer window and give The Microsoft Network some basic information about what your interests are. The Microsoft Network needs this information to add specific news and events related to your area, such as movie times and concerts, to your Custom Start Page. You also want to add several links to other sites on your Custom Start Page.

 TIP   If you don't want to customize your Start Page but still want to see some interesting links on the page, you can choose the Click Here button located under Don't Have Time To Create A Page Now? The Microsoft Network customizes your Start Page so that links to items such as news, Web sites, movie information, and a Web pick of the day are displayed.

Tell The Microsoft Network your personal preferences

In this exercise, you open The Microsoft Network home page and tell The Microsoft Network where you're located.

You can also click the MSN.com link on the Microsoft Internet Explorer Start Page.

1   Click in the Address box, type **www.msn.com** and then press ENTER.

2   At the top of The Microsoft Network Start Page, click the words "Create a Free Custom Start Page."

The MSN Custom Start Page changes frequently; therefore, the Custom Start Page link might not always be in the same location. You can usually find this link at the top of the page. When you click Custom Start Page, after a few moments the Custom Start Options page opens. Your screen should look similar to the following illustration.

You can also click the Customize My Page link at the bottom of your Start Page.

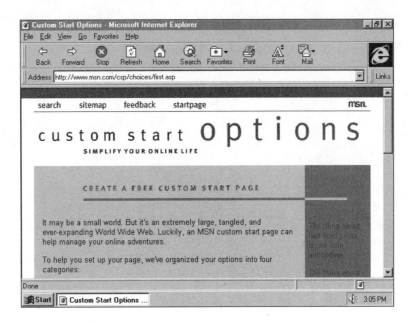

3 Scroll down, and under the words "Let's get customized!" click the Click Here button.

The Personal Preferences page opens. It might take the entire page several seconds to appear.

4 In the First Name box, type your first name. In the Last Name box, type your last name.

5 In the Address box, type your street address.

6 In the City box, type the full name of your city. In the State box, type your two-letter state abbreviation. In the ZIP Or Postal Code box, type your zip code or postal code.

 NOTE The Microsoft Network needs your address information so that the weather, movies, and television listings from the correct geographical area can be displayed.

If you want to receive messages from The Microsoft Network, select the Add Me To Your Mailing List For Announcements check box.

7 In the Select Your Time Zone area, select your time zone.

8 In the E-mail Address box, type your e-mail address.

If you are not sure that you have an e-mail account or what your e-mail address is, ask your system administrator.

9 If you want to create a Web link to The Microsoft Network section for kids, select the Please Put An Easy Link On My Page Especially For The Kids check box.

10   If you have a sound card installed and want to listen to music while you have your Custom Start Page displayed, select a MIDI music clip.

If you have a sound card but don't want music, select the None option; otherwise, the default music will play.

If a security message appears, click Yes.

11   Click the Setup This Page button.

The information you typed is saved on your hard disk, and the Services page opens.

Displaying Basic Services

Now that you have provided The Microsoft Network with some information, you can select the options you want to include on your Custom Start Page. Your first set of choices appears on the Services page. Services that you can choose from include links to MSN Investor, as well as to stocks, sports, movies, music, and family information.

Display basic services

While researching how to personalize your Custom Start Page, you decide to add some fun links to the page too. In this exercise, you add NFL and movie information to your Custom Start Page.

1   Scroll down, and under "Who's winning? Who's losing?" select the NFL check box.

2   Scroll down, and under "What's playing?" select the Movies check box.

If a security message appears, click Yes.

3   Click the Setup This Page button.

Your information has been saved. The News & Entertainment page opens.

 WEB PICK   Let Bill Nye show you the fun in science by visiting the Nye Labs and Bill Nye the Science Guy site. This is a great site for learning about the fundamentals of environmental science, chemistry, physics, biology, astronomy, and more. Visit it today at at http://nyelabs.kcts.org/

Selecting Art & Entertainment Site Categories

Using the Art & Entertainment page, you can select broad categories of sites that you want to display on your Custom Start Page. Categories include such topics as science & technology, world news, television listings, comic strips, politics, and even the weather. After you finish personalizing your Custom Start

Page, your category selections are displayed on your Custom Start Page as links to different MSN Web site pages. Each MSN page contains a list of links specific to that category. The Microsoft Network updates each category weekly; therefore, every week a new list of links is displayed and a whole new series of updated information is available. By displaying Art & Entertainment categories on your Custom Start Page, you can keep up-to-date on the latest news from around the world.

Select Art & Entertainment site categories

When you add a category to your Custom Start Page, the link under that category is updated weekly by The Microsoft Network.

As the person in charge of researching Internet Explorer, you decide to add a link to a Web site that will allow you to read articles about available Internet technology. In this exercise, you will add the Ziff-Davis Computer News link. Selecting this category displays links to computer magazines such as *PC Week*, *MacWeek*, and *PC Magazine*.

1 Scroll down, and under "Can't keep up with technology?" select the Ziff-Davis Computer News check box.

2 Click the Setup This Page button.

The information is saved. The Internet Searches page opens. You're almost done personalizing your Custom Start Page!

Selecting Search Options

Using the Internet Searches page, you can display search engines, display new sites on specific topics, as well as list your favorite links. *Search engines* are a handy feature that you can use to locate information on the Web about almost any topic. Using one of the search engines available to you, for instance, you can search for information about your favorite rock band, novelist, or vacation sites. Of course, you could do some research for work too. You'll learn more about search tools in Lesson 3.

WEB PICK To read cutting-edge computer and technology news and reviews, visit The Computer Network at http://www.cnet.com

Select search options

Being the employee in charge of researching Internet Explorer has some advantages. You get to use the cutting-edge technologies available on the Web and have fun while you work. You want your Custom Start Page to display new sites weekly on specific topics, including Computers & Technology, Art & Entertainment, and Fun & Interests. You also want to add a link to the Fitch & Mather home page.

*If you want
The Microsoft
Network to dis-
play a new Web
site every day,
select the Bring
Me A New Web
Site Every Day!
check box.*

1 Scroll down, and under "Let MSN show you some great sites," select the Computers & Technology check box, the Art & Entertainment check box, and the Fun & Interests check box.

2 Scroll down to the Keep Track of Your Favorite Links area. Under the URL heading, click the second down arrow, and then click http:// if necessary.

3 Click in the text box to the immediate right, and then type **www.microsoft.com/mspress/fnm**

4 Click the Site Name box, and then type **Fitch & Mather**

5 Click the Setup This Page button.

Your Custom Start Page opens. Scroll down, and your screen should look similar to the following illustration. Congratulations, you've just finished personalizing your Custom Start Page!

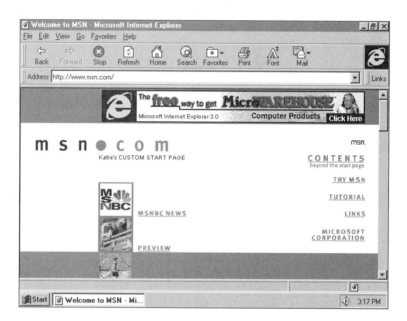

6 Click Yes.

 WEB PICK   Enjoy an irreverent look at the entertainment industry by visiting the Mr. Showbiz site at http://www.mrshowbiz.com

What's All This Talk About ActiveX?

ActiveX is the hot, new computer buzzword, but what is it? ActiveX is a new technology introduced by Microsoft. This clever innovation allows you to view special effects on the World Wide Web for a richer, more exciting Web experience, effects that you would not have been able to see two years ago. ActiveX has three components: ActiveX Controls, ActiveX Scripting, and ActiveX Documents.

Active X Controls are software plug-ins that run in Internet Explorer. A *webmaster*, a person who creates and maintains Web pages, can add an ActiveX Control to a Web page, and you can see the results when viewing the Web page in your Internet Explorer window. You don't need to do anything special to activate ActiveX; Internet Explorer gets your permission and downloads the software for you. When you don't need the software anymore, it's removed. ActiveX Controls can display simple effects such as a counter displaying the number of visits, a marquee scrolling across the page, an animation, or a Web page consisting of multiple frames without borders. To experience the versatility of ActiveX Controls, visit http://www.microsoft.com/activex/controls

ActiveX Scripting allows the browser to read and display pages that contain the most often used scripting languages. Using ActiveX Scripting, you can ask and answer questions, link to other programs, check data, and view Java applets and three-dimensional animations. For instance, you can go to one of the many online book companies and browse the books for sale, place orders, check the status of your order, and even cancel your order, without having to speak with a single person!

ActiveX Documents are the third handy component of ActiveX. Imagine opening a Microsoft Excel document in your Internet Explorer window and being able to display Excel's toolbars, menus, and interface—all without opening the program. A webmaster can use this feature to display an already existing file without having to add HTML code. This means that while you cruise the information superhighway, you can stop in the middle of the road to view non-HTML files, close them when you're finished, and then continue from the spot where you paused.

Another aspect of ActiveX is *Authenticode*, a new security technology that allows a webmaster to digitally sign the software code that you view. This signature is similar to the seal on a CD-ROM. When you buy a CD-ROM, you have to break open a seal that the manufacturer places on the package guaranteeing that the product hasn't been tampered with and that the CD-ROM is from the original manufacturer. When you visit a site that uses ActiveX Controls and you try to download from or upload to the site, Internet Explorer checks for the Authenticode. If the site has an Authenticode, a Windows Software Security dialog box appears displaying a certificate. If not, a message appears stating that the software hasn't been digitally signed and that the site is not guaranteed secure.

Saving Your Personalized Start Page as Your Custom Start Page

The Custom Start Page is a handy tool that helps you navigate the Web and locate other Web pages that might be of interest to you. But you're not limited to the Custom Start Page that automatically appears in your Internet Explorer window. You can use any other Web page that you like as your Start Page by changing the default to the new Web page.

 NOTE If you want to change any of your selections, scroll down to the section that you want to change, and then click the Options link on the left side of that section. The Custom Start Options page for that section opens. Make the changes you want, and then click the Setup This Page button. The changes are saved, and your Custom Start Page opens again.

Save your personalized page as your Custom Start Page

In this exercise, you save the page that you created as your Custom Start Page. When you do this, Internet Explorer automatically opens to this page every time you start the program and wherever you are on the Web, you can click the Home button and return to this page.

1   On the View menu, click Options.
2   In the Options dialog box, click the Navigation tab.
3   Be sure that Start Page is selected in the Page box.
4   Click Use Current, and then click OK.

The personalized page you created is saved as your Custom Start Page.

Where Did the World Wide Web Come From?

The World Wide Web was born at CERN, the European Laboratory for High Energy Physics, when scientists wanted a faster, more effective way to share research and late-breaking discoveries with other members of the scientific community. In 1989, Tim Berners-Lee, a computer specialist at CERN, and his colleague, Robert Cailliau, adapted a hypertext program that Berners-Lee had created for his own personal use. The formatting language (an early version of HTML) that Bernters-Lee and Cailliau developed made it possible for documents to be viewed over the Internet. These Web documents were very simple and only contained text. As HTML (the formatting language used to display Web pages) became more sophisticated, more elaborate Web pages became possible. Nowadays, Web pages can display pictures, video, and animation.

Restore the default Custom Start Page

If you get bored with your Custom Start Page, you can change it to yet another Web page, or you can restore your Internet Explorer Start Page. In this exercise, you will set your Start Page default back to the Internet Explorer Start Page.

1   On the View menu, click Options.

2   In the Options dialog box, click the Navigation tab.

3   Click Use Default, and then click OK.

4   Click the Home button to display the Internet Explorer Start Page.

Using Your Toolbars

To display the Quick Links toolbar, click the Links button to the right of the Address toolbar. The Quick Links toolbar appears, and the Address toolbar collapses to an Address button on the left.

Three toolbars are available by default in your Internet Explorer window: the Standard toolbar, the Address toolbar, and the Quick Links toolbar. You can use the buttons on the Standard toolbar to browse the Web. On each Standard toolbar button is a one-word explanation about what action that button performs. The address of the current Web page appears in the Address toolbar. Using the Address toolbar, you can also view the Web addresses of pages you visited recently, and you can return to a page by selecting the Web page address. The Quick Links toolbar, labeled Links in the Internet Explorer window, displays shortcuts to a variety of The Microsoft Network Web pages and to the Microsoft Web site.

 TIP   The Toolbar selection on the View menu is a toggle, or reversible, command. When you hide the toolbars, the check mark next to the word "Toolbar" disappears. To display the toolbars again, on the View menu, click Toolbar. The toolbars are displayed, and a check mark is added next to the word "Toolbar."

If your computer monitor has a small screen, however, the toolbars might interfere with Web page viewing. You can hide all the toolbars, hide specific toolbars, or move the toolbars around so that they occupy one line instead of two.

 WEB PICK   Learn more about PBS activities and get the scoop on upcoming programs by visiting The Public Broadcasting System site at http://www.pbs.org

Hide the toolbars

In this exercise, you want to hide the toolbars so that you can use the entire Internet Explorer window to view Web pages.

1   On the View menu, click Toolbar.

All three of your toolbars are hidden, and your window looks similar to the following illustration.

2   On the View menu, click Toolbar.

Your toolbars are displayed again.

Hide a toolbar

While using Internet Explorer, you find that you usually don't need the Quick Links toolbar. You'd rather see more of the computer screen, so you decide to hide the toolbar.

1   On the View menu, click Options.
2   In the Options dialog box, verify that the General tab is in front.
3   Under Toolbar, clear the Links check box, and then click OK.

Your Internet Explorer window appears without the Quick Links toolbar. Pretty handy feature, isn't it?

4   On the View menu, click Options.

5 On the General tab, select the Links check box.

6 Click OK.

Before you continue with the lesson, all your toolbars should be displayed.

 TIP If you want to remove the Address toolbar or the Standard toolbar, clear the Address check box or the Standard check box. You can also leave the Standard toolbar but remove the text that appears beneath each Standard toolbar item by clearing the Text Labels check box.

Move the toolbars

If you don't want to hide your toolbars, you can minimize the space they use by moving all three toolbars onto one line. In this exercise, you consolidate your toolbars on one line.

1 With your toolbars displayed, drag the Address section to the Standard toolbar.

2 Drag the Links section to the Standard toolbar.

The Address and Links sections of the toolbar appear on the same line as the icons, as shown in the following illustration.

Restore the toolbars

1 Drag the Address section down to restore the Address toolbar.

2 Drag the Links section down to restore the Quick Links toolbar.

Using Your Display Options

In addition to personalizing your Custom Start Page and moving your toolbars around, you can choose how Web pages appear in the Internet Explorer window. For instance, you can change your Internet Explorer default options so that pictures and multimedia files, such as sound files (.wav) and video files (.avi), are hidden. If you hide these files, when you open a Web page that includes multimedia files, icons are used as placeholders for the multimedia files. This change helps speed up the display of Web pages and is useful when you're concerned only about finding text information quickly. Another way to control your Web environment is by changing your display options so that all the link colors are the same, regardless of the colors designated by the Web site designer. You can also control the appearance of the fonts and toolbars

Displaying Multimedia Files

At Fitch & Mather, you have a 14,400 computer modem. Some of the Web pages you want to view download very slowly because they include a lot of graphics. The multimedia check boxes that control whether or not you see pictures and video and hear sound are selected by default. Viewing Web pages takes longer when a page contains numerous files, especially multimedia files. To speed up the browsing process, you decide to clear these options.

Why Are There Boxes on Web Pages Until the Graphics Appear?

Web page design must consider those people who are using older browsers that cannot display graphics. On these browsers, although the graphics are not visible, the page might be changed because of the space used by the "invisible" graphics. Web page designers add a placeholder that has descriptive text where the graphic would be to hold the graphic space. These placeholders are visible to all browsers, so before a graphic is loaded onto your computer, you will see its placeholder. Then, if your browser can display graphics, the placeholder is replaced on the Web page by the actual graphic. If your browser can't display graphics, you can still click the placeholder and jump to the appropriate page if the graphic is a link.

Hide multimedia files

1   On the View menu, click Options.

2   In the Options dialog box, be sure that the General tab is in front.

3   In the Multimedia area, clear the Show Pictures check box, the Play Sounds check box, and the Play Videos check box, and then click OK.

4   In the Address box, type **www.microsoft.com/mspress/fnm**

    The images on the Fitch & Mather page are replaced by placeholders.

 TIP   If the Show Pictures check box and Play Videos check box are cleared, you can still view a graphic. Use the right mouse button to click the picture or video placeholder, and then click Show Picture on the shortcut menu.

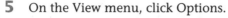

5 On the View menu, click Options.

6 Click the General tab; select the Show Pictures check box, the Play Sounds check box, and the Play Videos check box; and then click OK.

7 On the Standard toolbar, click the Refresh button.

The images are restored to the Fitch & Mather page.

8 Minimize the Internet Explorer window.

Changing the Color of Web Links

Web sites usually have links to other Web pages in the Web site. These links are displayed in colors, so you can easily distinguish links from basic text. Before you click the link, it appears in one color and after you have visited the link, it is in a different color. These colors are usually specified by the person who created the Web site, but if the colors are not specified, the links are in the default colors used by Internet Explorer: links are blue, links that have been selected are purple, text is black, and the window background is gray. You can change the links to any color available in your computer screen color palette.

Change the color of your Web links

1 On the Desktop, double-click My Computer, and then double-click the C drive.

2 Double-click the IE 3.0 SBS Practice folder, and then double-click the Glossary file.

3 On the View menu, click Options.

4 In the Options dialog box, make sure the General tab is in front.

5 Under Links, click the Visited box, and then select the color you want. Click OK.

The color palette closes.

6 Click the Unvisited box, select the color you want, and then click OK.

7 Click OK.

The color you selected is applied to your unvisited links.

TIP Using the General tab, you can also change the color of the text and the color of the background that appears in your Internet Explorer window. Keep in mind that these colors are defaults only—a Web page's predefined colors take precedence over these settings. Clear the Use Windows Color check box if it is selected. Click the Text box or Background box. Select the color you want to use, and then click OK.

45

Changing Your Web Text Fonts

Text on Web pages is usually displayed using proportional fonts. A *proportional font is a typeface in which each letter and the space between each letter is in* proportion to every other letter. For example, in proportional fonts, the L occupies less space than the W. In some instances, Web fonts are *fixed-width* or *monospace fonts*. Each fixed-width character occupies the same amount of space. For example, the letter L occupies the same amount of space as the letter W. Fixed-width fonts are usually used in tables where the text must be formatted a specific way. If you prefer to use a font other than the one displayed in the Internet Explorer window, you can change the fonts you want to use for your proportional and fixed-width fonts. Unless you install another fixed-width font, you can display fixed-width text only as Courier New.

 TIP Font size can be changed to make the text larger or smaller. You can change the size of the text by clicking the Font button on the Standard toolbar. Naturally, the larger the font size, the less text can fit on a line.

Change your proportional font

1   On the View menu, click Options.

2   On the General tab, click Font Settings.

    The Fonts dialog box appears.

3   Click the Proportional Font down arrow, and then select the font you want to use.

4   Click Apply.

    The selected font is applied to your text.

Customizing Your History Folder

Did you know that you can control how long Web addresses remain in the History folder? Well, you can, and you can even clear the History folder entirely. By default, Internet Explorer keeps the addresses of the Web pages you visited for 20 days, and then automatically removes them. If you want to remove addresses before the 20 days are up, you can clear them yourself.

Select the number of days to keep addresses

1   In the Options dialog box, click the Navigation tab.

2   Under History, click the Number Of Days To Keep Pages In History up arrow to increase the number of days, or click the down arrow to decrease the number of days.

3   Click OK.

The Options dialog box closes.

TIP   You can view the contents of the History folder by clicking the View History button on the Navigation tab.

Clear the History folder

IMPORTANT   When you clear the History folder, you are removing all the Web pages from your History folder. If you do not want to remove any Web pages from your History folder, do not perform this exercise.

1   On the View menu, click Options.

2   Click the Navigation tab, and then click Clear History.

A message appears asking you to confirm that you want to delete all items in your History folder.

3   Click Yes.

4   Click OK.

Your History folder is emptied, and the Options dialog box closes.

Changing a Web Graphic into Desktop Wallpaper

The background pattern and color of your Desktop are usually referred to as *wallpaper*. Wallpaper is a feature that you can use to liven up your computer environment. You can use wallpaper to display your favorite photos and images, or you can create an entire theme to coordinate your wallpaper, mouse pointer, and computer sounds. You can select from the different types of wallpaper available in Windows 95 or Windows NT by using Control Panel. However, you're not limited by the wallpaper available in your operating system—now you can create unusual and colorful wallpaper by using Web graphics. Any graphic on the Web can be used as wallpaper. For instance, a picture, an animation, or a video can be used. Remember, however, that if you use an animation or a video, only one frame, or single still image, of the file can be used as wallpaper; therefore, you will not see any movement.

Change a Web graphic into Desktop wallpaper

The Fitch & Mather company logo was changed recently. You like the new logo and want to convert the image into wallpaper. In this exercise, you will convert the Fitch & Mather logo into wallpaper for your Desktop.

1 In the Address box, type **www.microsoft.com/mspress/fnm/** and then press ENTER.

2 Use the right mouse button to click the Fitch & Mather Web logo.

A shortcut menu opens.

3 Click Set As Wallpaper.

The Fitch & Mather Web logo is now your Desktop wallpaper.

4 Click the Minimize button to view the wallpaper.

Your screen should look like the following illustration.

Restore your original wallpaper

1 On the taskbar, click Start, point to Settings, and then click Control Panel.

2 Double-click the Display icon.

The Display Properties dialog box appears.

3 In the Wallpaper box, use the arrows to scroll through the list.

4 Select the wallpaper you want to display, and then click OK.

NOTE If you'd like to build on the skills that you learned in this lesson, you can do the One Step Further. Otherwise, skip to "Finish the lesson."

One Step Further: Changing Your Privacy Settings to Protect Your Computer

Many Web sites are set up in such a way that unauthorized users can't get access to the data being sent to or sent from the site. These sites are called *secure sites*. Using Internet Explorer, you can safely send data to and receive data from secure sites. You can set up a privacy setting in Internet Explorer so that you will be warned when you are sending information to an unsecure Web page and when a site is downloading information to your computer without your knowledge. For instance, you can be warned when you are about to transmit credit card information over an unsecured line or when the site is downloading "cookies" to your computer. *Cookies* refers to the pieces of information that a Web site downloads to your computer and uses to customize your viewing of the Web site. The concern, of course, is that a file is being downloaded to your computer, and you don't know what that file contains.

Microsoft Internet Explorer has an Internet security feature known as a *certificate*. Organizations that have secure Web sites are issued certificates for a set period of time. When you view that organization's Web site, Internet Explorer verifies that the certificate hasn't expired and, therefore, that the site is still secure.

When you send and receive information, you risk downloading cookies or viruses, or otherwise exposing your computer to unsecure sites. Viewing Web pages doesn't usually pose any risks to your computer, but when you download a file (take a file from the Web and put it on your hard disk), you can expose your computer to a virus. A computer virus is a software program that infects your files. A virus can do something silly, such as make a message appear on your screen, or it can destroy your files.

Files available in Internet service provider areas, such as newsgroups on The Microsoft Network, are scanned before they are made accessible to users. Individuals who put files on the Web usually try to ensure that their files are clean. But every now and then, an infected file gets through. Cookies will not hurt your files. Some viruses are also benign; others can cause serious damage.

> ### *Protecting Your Computer*
> You can use your Microsoft Internet Explorer options to change the number of warnings you receive when you download files or expose your computer to security risks. Weigh the number of security warnings you set up against your desire for rapid sending and receiving of information.

Choose your privacy settings

1   On the View menu, click Options.

2   Click the Advanced tab.

3   Under Warnings, be sure that the Warn Before Sending Over An Open Connection check box is selected, and then choose the Always option.

    This selection tells Internet Explorer that you always want to be warned before you send information to an unsecure Internet site.

4   Be sure that the Warn If Changing Between Secure And Unsecure Mode check box is selected to be warned before you try to view unsecure Web pages.

5   Be sure that the Warn About Invalid Site Certificates check box is selected to be warned before you send information to a site whose security certificate has expired.

6   Select the Warn Before Accepting "Cookies" check box to be warned before receiving a cookie from an Internet site.

7   Click OK.

Finish the lesson

1   To continue to the next lesson, on the toolbar click the Home button.

2   If you are finished using Internet Explorer for now, on the File menu, click Close.

3   Close all open windows.

Lesson Summary

To	Do this
Tell The Microsoft Network your personal preferences	Scroll down from the top of the page, click Create A Free Custom Start Page, and then click Customize Now! Type your name, street address, and e-mail address. Select a time zone. Select any options that you want to display on your Custom Start Page. Click the Setup This Page button.
Display services	Scroll down, and then select the options you want to display on your Custom Start Page. Click the Setup This Page button.

To	Do this
Select site categories	Scroll down, and then select the options you want. Click the Setup This Page button.
Select search options	Scroll down, and then select the options you want to display. Click the Setup This Page button.
Use a different page as your Start Page	Display the Web page in the Internet Explorer window. On the View menu, click Options, and then click the Navigation tab. Click Use Current, and then click OK.
Restore your Custom Start Page	On the View menu, click Options, and then click the Navigation tab. Click Use Default, and then click OK.
Hide all the toolbars	On the View menu, click Toolbar to clear the check mark.
Hide a toolbar	On the View menu, click Options, and then click the General tab. Under Toolbars, clear the check box for the toolbar you want to hide, and then click OK.
Move a toolbar	Drag the toolbar to the new location.
Hide multimedia files	On the View menu, click Options, and then click the General tab. Under Multimedia, clear the check box of the file type you don't want to display, and then click OK.
Change your Web link colors	On the View menu, click Options, and then click the General tab. Under Appearance, click the box beside the link you want to change, select a color, and then click OK.
Change your proportional fonts	On the View menu, click Options, and then click the General tab. Under Fonts, click the Proportional Fonts down arrow, select a font, and then click OK.

To	Do this
Change your fixed-width font	On the View menu, click Options, and then click the General tab. Under Fonts, click the Fixed-Width Font down arrow, select a font, and then click OK.
Select the number of days to keep Web addresses in the History folder	On the View menu, click Options, and then click the Navigation tab. Click the Number Of Days To Keep Pages In History up arrow or down arrow, and then click OK.
Clear the Web addresses in the History folder	On the View menu, click Options, and then click the Navigation tab. Click Clear History, click Yes, and then click OK.
Change a graphic into Desktop wallpaper	Use the right mouse button to select the image, and then click Set As Wallpaper on the shortcut menu.

For online information about	On the Help menu, click Help Topics. In the Help Topics dialog box, click Index, and then type
Changing and returning to the Start Page	**Start Page** or **home page,** and then display Changing or Returning to
Reorganizing the toolbar	**toolbar,** and then display Changing the appearance of
Hiding Web page files	**hiding,** and then display Animations and pictures, to display pages faster
Changing fonts	**fonts**
Changing link colors	**hyperlinks,** and then display Changing the color of
Setting up the History folder	**history list**
Changing Web graphics into Desktop wallpaper	**wallpaper** or **graphics,** and then display Using a graphic image as Desktop wallpaper

Searching
the Web

Estimated time
30 min.

In this lesson you will learn how to:

- Search for information on a Web page.
- Search for information on the World Wide Web.
- Modify search options to narrow a search.
- Save search results.

With the millions of Web pages on the World Wide Web, it can be overwhelming to try to find the specific information you want. Several sources, such as trade magazines, advertisements, and television commercials, include the Uniform Resource Locators (URLs), or addresses, for specific Web sites; but when you think about how much information is on the Web, you can see that these sources can only skim the surface of the information available. So how do you find information on the Web? For example, if you wanted to find information about computers, where would you start? And if you don't know the URL of a Web site, how can you open the page to view the information? The answer is that you need to search for pages about the topic you're interested in. In this lesson, you learn to use a tool—the search engine—that will help you find what you want on the World Wide Web.

In your job at Fitch & Mather, you have been assigned a new account: Awesome Computers' new finger-held mouse. You decide to search the WWW for information about Frank Lloyd Wright, because you are thinking of using the theme of innovation in your ad design.

Finding Information on the Web

One of the greatest benefits of the Web is that it is a huge resource of information about a multitude of different topics. But this benefit can also be a hindrance, because it can be difficult to find specific information on a topic.

When the Internet was first created, there was no thought to organizing information for easy accessibility. The Internet was a hodgepodge of information created by people who had little in common except that they put information on and took information off the Internet. Rarely would Internet users browse unfamiliar addresses. At that time, creating a computerized method of finding Web pages about a particular topic wasn't feasible because computer technology was not nearly advanced enough to support such a memory-consuming system.

When computer technology progressed enough to handle the memory requirements of such a system, the challenge was to develop a way to find Web pages without knowing their addresses. These Web pages were located at different sites, were created on different types of computers, and were created by using different programs.

Typically the actual process that search engines use to search their databases is proprietary, so only those who designed a search engine can truly know how that engine works.

The response: Several companies developed systems that can store copies of Web page text in huge central databases. These databases also contain indexes of most or all of the text in each of the Web pages stored within it. Special programs called *crawlers* or *spiders*, so known because they "crawl" around the database, were created to search these indexes for information. If you, for example, want to find information about computers, a crawler looks through the index and finds the Web pages that contain the word "computer." A list of the search results is then generated. The huge database that contains the text of Web pages, the Web page index, and the crawlers that search the index are, together, a *search engine*.

There are several search engines available on the Internet. Each search engine has its own Web site, so all you need to know to use the engine is its address. All search engines are not, however, the same, and there are methods of using a search engine that will make your efforts easier and more successful.

Selecting the Most Efficient Search Method

Each search engine was designed by different people for different purposes, and so the various engines find information in different ways.

Information available on the Internet can be stored in more than one search engine database, but no search engine stores all the Web pages. One search engine might find more or fewer Web pages in a search than another search engine, and one search engine might find slightly different types of information than another search engine. The following table lists the major search engines, and each one's basic method of operation.

	Search engine name	Internet address	How it works
It is not unusual for a search engine to contain over 30 gigabytes of stored information. A typical hard disk in your computer can hold between 100 megabytes and 2.2 gigabytes.	AltaVista	http://www.altavista.digital.com/	Searches its database of individual Web pages for words or phrases you enter.
	Excite	http://www.excite.com	Searches for Web pages and concepts in the Web pages. Catalogs sites, and provides reviews of cataloged sites. Also searches newsgroups and classified ads (see Lesson 5, "Communicating Through Newsgroups," for more information).
	Infoseek	http://www.infoseek.com	Searches its database of individual Web pages, and displays an excerpt for each page that matches your search criteria. Also searches Usenet newsgroups, sites selected as good sites by Infoseek, e-mail addresses, news stories, and FAQ (Frequently Asked Questions) Web pages.
	Lycos	http://www.lycos.com	Searches its database of individual Web pages, and then provides an outline and abstract for each page that matches your search criteria.
	Magellan	http://www.mckinley.com	Searches its database of individually reviewed and rated Web sites. Provides a summary and a link to the full review of the site for each site that matches your search criteria.
	Yahoo!	http://www.yahoo.com	Searches its database of sites, and organizes them by category. When a site that matches your search criteria is found, a summary of the site and a link to the site category are displayed. Identifies and rates new, cool, pick of the week, and other noteworthy sites.

Other search engines include HotBot, DejaNews, WebCrawler, Open Text, NlightN, Cosmix Motherload, Savvy Search, Metacrawler, Internet Sleuth, Honda Super Search, and Search.com. You can use one of the search engines in the table on the previous page to find any of these search engines.

NOTE As you use the different search engines, you will probably find that you like one or two better than the others. Choosing a favorite search engine is entirely a matter of personal taste. The search engines search for and present information in different ways. Try them all to see which best suits your needs.

How Do Search Engines Find New Web Pages?

Some Web page information is added to search engine databases by the creator of the Web site, but other information is added to the database automatically by crawlers which, instead of searching a database for information, search the Internet, going from page to page looking for ones that are new. Crawlers follow the links of one page to another page, and if that page is not in the database, the crawler adds the page. A crawler continuously searches Web pages for new links to add to its database, so the information available on a search engine can change from one week to the next.

All the URLs, and sometimes other information, such as the title of the Web page, are indexed in the search engine database, just as a book is indexed. Each search engine indexes its database differently, and each search engine examines its database for different information. The two most common ways that a search engine looks for matches to your search are by *keywords* or by *concept*. When a search engine looks for keywords, it scans the Web pages in its database for exact matches to the text that you entered for the search. When a search engine looks for a concept, it scans the Web pages in its database for any pages that discuss the subject of the text you entered for the search. For example, if you look for information about a computer mouse in Lycos and then in Excite, Lycos returns a list of Web sites that contain the exact words "computer" and "mouse." If the Web site doesn't contain those exact words, or if words are misspelled, the site will not appear in the list. Excite, on the other hand, returns a list of Web sites that are conceptually about a computer mouse.

TIP Some Internet service providers charge hourly rates for their services. If you are using one of these providers, you might want to read through this lesson before starting the exercises. This will minimize the amount of time you spend connected to your service provider.

Start Internet Explorer

IMPORTANT To successfully complete this lesson, you will need to have a computer, a modem, and a dial-up connection to an Internet service provider or a connection to the Internet through a network. In addition, you must have Internet Explorer 3.0 installed.

1 On the Desktop, double-click The Internet icon.

The Internet Explorer window opens, and the Microsoft Network Sign In dialog box appears. If you have not installed The Microsoft Network, a dialog box appears asking if you want to install MSN.

2 In the Member ID box, type your Member ID.

This is the name you gave yourself when you set up The Microsoft Network.

3 In the Password box, type your password.

If you don't want to type your password every time you connect to The Microsoft Network, click the Remember My Password check box. Use caution if you choose this option, because then anyone using MSN on your computer has access to your MSN account.

4 Click Connect.

After a few moments, The Microsoft Network window and the MSN To-day window open. If you are using a modem, on the taskbar you will see a small modem icon in the status box.

Modem icon

TROUBLESHOOTING If you cannot connect to The Microsoft Network, try the following: check your modem settings, verify that your modem is turned on (if it is an external modem) and connected to a phone jack, and check that you are using the correct phone number.

5 Maximize the Internet Explorer window.

The Internet Explorer window expands to fill the entire screen. After a few moments, a page on the World Wide Web appears.

Starting the Search

The search engine builds a list of Web page titles based on its search for the word or phrase you entered in its Search box. The Web pages in the search engine's database that most exactly match the word or phrase that you entered will be listed first, sometimes with a percentage next to their titles. These percentages are called *confidence scores*. Confidence scores rate how well the results of the search match the text you entered. If the highest ranked Web page match is below 50 percent, you should reevaluate your search text.

The format of the list of results is determined by the search engine you are using. For example, Excite gives a list of matching Web pages with a confidence score and a summary of the information on the Web page, while AltaVista gives a list of matching titles of Web pages with a couple lines of the text on the Web page. Regardless of which search engine you use, the list of results will contain links to each of the pages that the search engine found. All you have to do is click a link, and you are on your way to a new Web page.

 TIP Search engine databases are only as good as the text on the Web pages they include. If text on a Web page is misspelled, a search will not acknowledge that it matches the search results you want. If you cannot find a specific Web page, try misspelling a keyword, and then see if the search engine gives you a search result. For more information about each search engine, look at its home page. The home page usually contains a link to information about how to search.

When you use a search engine to find information on the Web, you need to enter text into the Search box that will help you find what you are looking for. The more specific you can be, the more closely the search results will match your requested topic. For example, if you searched for "computers," the search result would include information about everything to do with a computer or all sites that include the word "computer" in their text; if you searched for "computer mouse," the search result would include information related only to a computer mouse or sites that include the words "computer mouse" in their text.

In the exercises in this lesson, you use the Excite search engine to find information about Frank Lloyd Wright, since you are thinking about using photos of some of his architecture in the Amazing Mouse campaign.

 WEB PICK Search for answers to your health questions by visiting http://www.housecall.com

*What Is the Best Way to Search
with a Particular Search Engine?*

Each search engine has a search technique that works best with it. The following table explains the best techniques for six of the most popular search engines.

Search engine	How to search
AltaVista	Searches by keywords and phrases. Be as specific as possible. Type your request carefully; AltaVista is case-sensitive (that is, an uppercase W, for example, is not recognized as being the same as a lowercase w). Use quotation marks to link words together for more specific searches. For example, if you want to search for information about North Africa, type "North Africa." The quotation marks connect "North" and "Africa" together so that the search engine looks for sites that include the two words next to each other.
Excite	Searches by keyword or by concept. Type the words that you want to find; the more words you use, the more focused your request is. You can even phrase your request in the form of a question. Excite searches for sites that contain at least one of the words you type. Click the Find Similar link located next to each search result to help you find Web pages similar to one found in a search. You can also browse through Excite-reviewed Web pages.
Infoseek	Searches by keywords or phrases. Be as specific as possible; Infoseek is case-sensitive. Use quotation marks to link words together for more specific searches. You can also browse through the topics listed on the Infoseek home page.
Lycos	Searches by keywords. Be as specific as possible; Lycos is case-sensitive. Use quotation marks to link words together for more specific searches. Do not use arabic numbers, such as 1 or 244, in your search. You can also browse through several topics listed on the Lycos home page.
Magellan	Searches by keywords. Be as specific as possible. You can also browse through several topics listed on the Magellan home page.
Yahoo!	Searches by keywords. Enter a few keywords. Yahoo! will search categories, titles, and comments to find matching words. You can also browse through several topics listed on the Yahoo! home page.

Using Concepts to Search for Web Pages

As mentioned earlier in this lesson, there are two ways that search engines search their databases for matching Web pages. The first type is by concept. "By concept" means that a search engine not only finds any Web pages that contain the words that you type in the Search box, but also finds any Web pages that discuss the idea of what you type in the Search box. For example, if you search for "computer hardware," you will not only get Web pages with "computer hardware" in their titles, but Web pages that discuss various types of computer hardware. Searching by concept typically gives you a large selection of matching Web pages. Using a by concept search, you may find links to Web pages containing topics you would not have thought of searching for.

Search for Web pages by concept

In the following exercise, you search by concept for Web pages about American architects.

You can
also type
home.microsoft
.com/access/
allinone.asp in
the Address box,
and press ENTER.

1   On the toolbar, click the Search button to open the Find It Fast page.

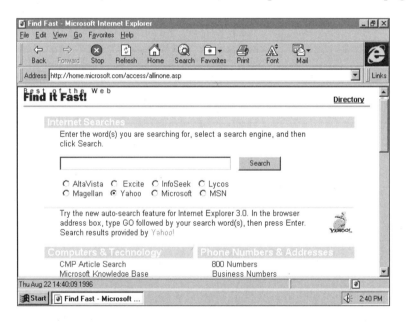

By default,
Excite searches
by concept.

If a security
message
appears,
click Yes.

2   Type **American architects,** click the Excite option to select it, and then click the Search button next to the Search box.

Excite scans each of the Web pages in its extensive database for those Web pages that contain the desired concept—in this case, American architects. After a moment, the Excite Search Results page opens with a list of the top 10 of the several million documents that match your search criteria.

3   Scroll down to the beginning of the list of search results.

A statement preceding the list indicates that documents 1-10 of approximately three million matches are listed below. This search result is too large; it is almost impossible to know where to start. The top 10 are identified by the confidence scores given next to each Web page title listed. None of the top 10 Web sites even mentions Frank Lloyd Wright, so the choice of search words was not specific enough.

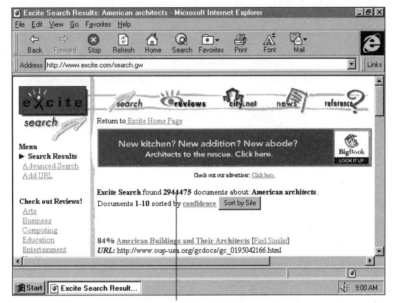

Number of Web pages
that match your search

 IMPORTANT   Because the information on the WWW is so dynamic, the search results you receive might be different from those in the illustrations of this book.

Narrowing Your Search Options

Sometimes, your search still results in too many Web pages to sort through, as it did when you searched for American architects. You can refine your search to be more specific so that fewer Web sites are found. The more specific you get about the Web pages you are looking for, the fewer Web pages you will have to search.

Refine the search terms

In this exercise, you use the Excite search engine to refine your search so that you can find more specific information about Frank Lloyd Wright.

1　At the bottom of the Excite Search Results page, click the Advanced Search link.

The Advanced Excite Search Features page opens.

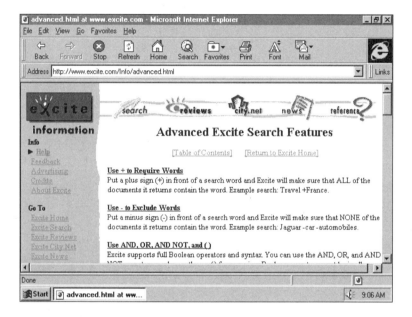

2　Scroll down, click in the What box, and then type **Frank Lloyd Wright**

If a security message appears, click Yes.

3　Click the Search button.

After a few moments, the Excite Search Results page opens, listing the top 10 Web sites that match your refined search. If you scroll down to the top of the search results list, you will see that the number of matching sites has been reduced to about a million. Now Frank Lloyd Wright appears in the title of some of the matches, but there are still a lot of choices. So many matches remain because Excite is searching for Web sites that include the words Frank or Lloyd or Wright in any combination or order. If you click the Next Document button a few times, you will see that there is a variety of different subjects included in this search.

Continue to narrow the search

If a security message appears, click Yes.

1 On the Excite Web page, click the Advanced Search link.

The Advanced Excite Search Features page opens.

2 Scroll down, click in the What box, type **+Frank +Lloyd +Wright +architecture** and then click Search.

The Excite Search Results page opens. The pluses tell the search engine to connect all the words together, so that only those Web pages that contain a matching concept or match of all those words will be returned.

3 Scroll to the top of the list.

The number of matching documents is greatly reduced, and all the top 10 matches contain information on Frank Lloyd Wright architecture.

4 Click the top Web page match.

The Web page opens. You should find information on Frank Lloyd Wright architecture or a link to a page that includes information on Frank Lloyd Wright architecture.

For more information about using advanced search features in Excite, go to www.excite.com/Info/advanced.html

WEB PICK For lots of cool stuff about today's most popular computer games, try http://www.gamespot.com

Using Keywords to Find a Page

Searching for a concept can give you many different Web pages to view, and might return some unexpected Web pages, but frequently you want to find Web pages that contain specific words. Searching for keywords helps narrow the search to Web pages that contain the words you want to search for, not just the concepts behind them.

Yahoo! searches only for keywords.

Search for Web pages by keywords

In the following exercise, you do a keyword search using the Yahoo! search engine.

You can also click the Search button on the toolbar, and continue at step 2.

1 In the Address box, type **www.yahoo.com** and then press ENTER.

The Yahoo! search engine home page opens.

If a security message appears, click Yes.

WEB PICK For news about a variety of subjects, including sports, games, and personal finance, visit the Pathfinder Web site at http://www.pathfinder.com

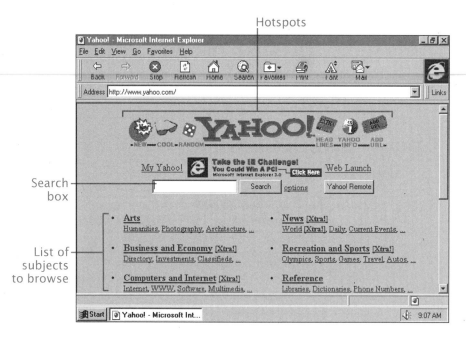

2   In the Search box, type **Frank Lloyd Wright**, and press ENTER.

Yahoo! scans each of the Web pages in its extensive database for those Web pages that contain the keywords, Frank Lloyd Wright. After a moment, the Yahoo! Search Results Web page opens, displaying matches 1-25. This list does not contain a confidence score. Yahoo! does not use confidence scores.

Exploring Search Results

After you've gotten search results, you might need to do more searching than just clicking a link to a Web page. Sometimes there is no exact match for the word or phrase you entered, or your subject might have many different layers of search results that you should explore, depending on what you are specifically looking for. For example, in Yahoo!, if you enter the keywords "computer mouse," Yahoo! returns a search result of topic lists that include those keywords, along with Web sites that include the keywords. When you receive a list of subjects, you must click a subject link to see whether the information you want is there or whether you have to continue your search.

Once you find the site you have been searching for, you might want to save it for future reference. You can use the Favorites folder to save a Web page you have found after a search.

You have heard from a co-worker, who is a fan of Frank Lloyd Wright, that NASA has a great Web site on the architect, called the Frank Lloyd Wright Pages. In these exercises, you explore a search link to find this great site, and then save the site in your Favorites folder.

Explore a search link

NOTE Because the information on the WWW is so dynamic, the search results you receive may be different from those in the illustrations of this book.

1 Scroll down, and then click the Arts: Architecture: Architects: Masters: Wright, Frank Lloyd (1867–1959) link.

The Yahoo! Arts: Architecture: Architects: Masters Web page opens. This page has a more specific list of Web sites.

2 Scroll down, and then click the Frank Lloyd Wright [nasa.gov] link.

The Frank Lloyd Wright Pages home page opens.

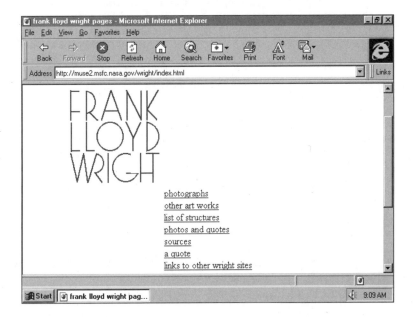

Save a search

1 On the toolbar, click the Favorites button, and then click Add To Favorites.

The Add To Favorites dialog box appears.

2 Click OK.

The Frank Lloyd Wright Pages home page is saved to your Favorites folder.

WEB PICK   Visit The New York Stock Exchange Web site, and find out what the bulls and the bears are up to at http://www.nyse.com

Searching the Internet, Not Just the Web

See Lesson 1, "Traveling the World Wide Web," for more information about service types.

Not all of the information on the Internet is accessible through the Web, so not all of the information available on the Internet is indexed in the Web search engines. Other Internet services will give you access to this information. One such Internet service is Gopher. *Gopher* is a text-only service that uses a menu system to list Internet resources. Because Gopher doesn't have any graphics, it is faster than most Web search engines. Gopher has its own search engines, which search different hosts for the information you are looking for.

Although the results of a Gopher search might not be as large as the results of a Web search engine, using a Gopher search engine, you can often find articles that you cannot find when you use a Web search engine.

Search for information using Gopher

Some Gopher directories have restrictions on who can use them. If you have difficulty opening a Gopher directory, try another.

As part of your research for ideas for the ad campaign for Awesome Computers, you decide to do some research on ergonomics to get a clear idea of the benefits of using a mouse specifically engineered to minimize wrist problems. In this exercise, you decide to use Gopher to search for information about ergonomics.

 NOTE   If a message from Microsoft Internet Explorer says it cannot open the Internet site, click OK. The directory should still open even though you received an error message.

1   In the Address box, type **gopher://gopher.tc.umn.edu** and press ENTER.

The Gopher root directory at University of Minnesota opens. The University of Minnesota created Gopher and is the access point to the Gopherspace search engines. Your screen should look like the following illustration.

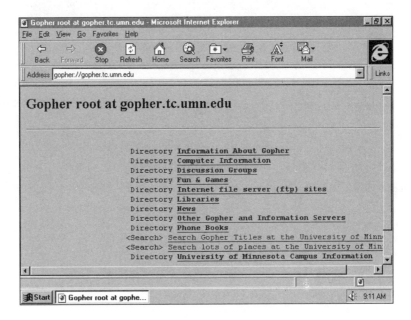

2 Click the Other Gophers And Information Servers link.

The Gopher Directory At gopher.tc.umn.edu opens.

3 Click the Search Titles In Gopherspace Using Veronica link.

The Gopher Directory At gopher.tc.umn.edu opens. Veronica is one of the best Gopherspace search engines. Veronica stands for **V**ery **E**asy **Ro**dent-**O**riented **N**et-wide **I**ndex to **C**omputerized **A**rchives. Rodents are the Internet equivalent to Web crawlers. Veronica searches for a directory or document title that includes the words you want to find.

4 Click the Find GOPHER DIRECTORIES By Title Words (Via PSINet) link.

The Gopher Index Search–veronica.psi.net page opens.

Veronica is not case-sensitive.

5 Click in the box, type **ergonomics** and press ENTER.

The Gopher Directory At veronica.psi.net page opens with a list of directories that deal with the subject of ergonomics.

6   Click a link that interests you.

Another directory or a Gopher document opens.

 NOTE   If you'd like to build on the skills that you learned in this lesson, you can do the One Step Further. Otherwise, skip to "Finish the lesson."

One Step Further: Restricting Access to the Internet

Many people are concerned about the content of Web pages. Virtually anyone with access to the Internet can view Web pages that contain adult content, no matter how young that person is. As a response to this concern, a rating system has been created by the creators of Web pages. Purely voluntary, this system rates Web sites for language, nudity, sex, and violence. This ratings chart is being used by more and more Web site creators as the concern for Web page content increases. You can change the settings of your computer so that if you or anyone using your computer attempts to open a Web site with an adult rating, the site cannot be viewed, unless the correct password is typed. Only Web sites that have been rated can be screened.

Control access to Web pages

In the following exercise, you set up Internet Explorer to view ratings.

1   On the View menu, click Options.

The Options dialog box appears.

2   Click the Security tab.

3   Click the Settings button.

The Create Supervisor Password dialog box appears.

4   Type a password in the Password box, press TAB, and type the password again. Click OK.

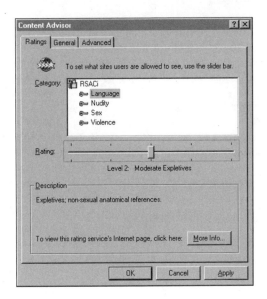

5   In the Category box, click Language.

The Content Advisor dialog box appears. This is where you control the level of the language, nudity, sex, or violence that the person using Internet Explorer is allowed to see.

A Ratings slide rule appears beneath the Category box. You are only setting ratings for acceptable language. Each category has to be set separately. The options range from Inoffensive Slang to Explicit Or Crude Language.

TIP   For more specific information on what each of the different levels includes in the way of language, nudity, sex, or violence, click More Info at the bottom of the Content Advisor dialog box. You must be online when you do this, because the Web site for the Recreational Software Advisory Council is opened for you to view.

6   Drag the slider bar to the rating you want.

The description beneath the Rating slide rule changes. As you move the slider bar from rating to rating on the slide rule, a description of the blocked language appears in the Description area below.

7   Select any other category of concern, and repeat step 6.

NOTE If you want to bypass the restrictions to Web pages that you have set for other users of Internet Explorer, click the General tab, and then select the Supervisor Can Type A Password To Allow Users To View Restricted Content box.

8 Click OK.

The ratings are set. The Ratings Monitor is automatically turned on after you set up the ratings.

Turn off Ratings Monitor

1 Click the Disable Ratings button.

The Supervisor Password dialog box appears.

2 Enter your password, and then click OK.

A Content Advisor dialog box appears with a message that the Content Advisor has been turned off.

3 Click OK.

The Content Advisor dialog box closes.

4 Click OK.

The Options dialog box closes.

 WEB PICK Download free or low-cost software programs, when you visit http://www.windows95.com

Finish the lesson

1 To continue to the next lesson, on the toolbar, click the Home button.

2 If you are finished using Internet Explorer for now, on the File menu, click Close.

The Microsoft Network dialog box appears.

3 Close all open windows.

Lesson Summary

To	Do this	Button
Search for information by concept	Click the Search button. Select a search engine that searches by concept, type the information you want to search for, and then click Search.	Search
Refine the search terms	Type more specific information in the Search box, and then click Search.	
Use keywords to find a page	Select a search engine that searches by keyword. In the Search box, type words you want to search for. Click Search.	
Explore a search result	Click a link in the list, and see if it contains the information you want.	

For online information about	On the Help menu, click Help Topics. In the Help Topics dialog box, click Index, and then type
Searching for information	**searching**, and then display the Internet by concept
Refining search terms	Go to the search engine Help page for specific help.
Using keywords	Go to the search engine Help page for specific help.

Review & Practice

Estimated time
35 min.

- Open and browse a Web site.
- Add a Web site to your Favorites folder.
- Print a Web page.
- Change your Custom Start Page to a different Web page.
- Move your toolbars.
- Change your History folder settings.
- Use a search engine to locate information on the Web.

Before you move on to Part 2, which covers communicating over the Internet using e-mail, newsgroups, and NetMeeting, you can practice the skills you learned in Part 1 by working through this Review & Practice section. You'll open Internet Explorer, open and browse a Web site, save and view a Web page, change your Start Page, and search for information on the Internet. In addition, you will add a Web page to your Favorites folder and then print the page.

Scenario

As part of your job at a large environmental engineering company, you've just been assigned the task of hiring an advertising agency. This agency should have an excellent reputation and be large enough to handle your company's account. A friend told you about Fitch & Mather, but you would like to find more information about the company before you contact them. You know Fitch & Mather has a Web site, so you decide to read about the company on the Internet first.

Step 1: Open and Browse a Web Site

Now that you've been assigned the task of hiring an advertising agency, you want to browse the Fitch & Mather Web site.

1 Start Internet Explorer.
2 Open the Fitch & Mather home page at www.microsoft.com/mspress/fnm
3 Using links, display the Our Clients page.
4 Return to the Fitch & Mather home page.

For more information about	See
Starting Internet Explorer	Lesson 1
Opening a specific Web page	Lesson 1
Browsing Web pages	Lesson 1
Using links to navigate	Lesson 1

Step 2: Add a Favorite Web Page and Print the Page

The Fitch & Mather Web site contains some helpful information about the company. You want to keep the Fitch & Mather home page address in a folder called Agencies which will be located within your Favorites folder. You also want to print a copy of the Fitch & Mather introduction page so that you can show the information to your supervisor.

1 Open the Favorites folder.
2 Create a new Favorites folder called Agencies.
3 Add the Fitch & Mather home page to your Agencies folder, and close the Favorites window.
4 Print the page.

For more information about	See
Adding a Web page to the Favorites folder	Lesson 1
Opening a Web page in the Favorites folder	Lesson 1
Printing a Web page	Lesson 2

Step 3: *Change Your Custom Start Page to Another Web Page*

You decide to change your Start Page to the Fitch & Mather home page. You like the company and want to keep tabs on the company's announcements and portfolio. When you have made your hiring decision, you want to change your Start Page back to your Custom Start Page.

1 Open the Options dialog box.

2 Make the Fitch & Mather home page your Start Page.

For more information about	See
Opening the Custom Start Page	Lesson 2
Modifying the Custom Start Page	Lesson 2
Changing your Start Page to another Web page	Lesson 2
Changing your Start Page back to your Custom Start Page	Lesson 2

Step 4: *Move Your Toolbars*

You haven't been exploring the Web for very long, but you are beginning to think that your toolbars are distracting you from the Web pages that appear in your Internet Explorer window. You decide that you want to display your toolbars on one line.

1 Move the Quick Links and Address toolbars to the same line as the Standard toolbar.

2 Restore the toolbars by moving them back to their previous positions.

For more information about	See
Working with toolbars	Lesson 2
Browsing Web pages	Lesson 1

Step 5: *Modify Your History Folder*

When you open the History folder, you see that a lot of Web pages are stored here. You want to reduce the number of days that the History folder stores viewed Web pages and clear the History folder of all the pages stored.

1 Open the Options dialog box.

2 Change the number of days you want to keep pages in the History folder.

3 If you want to, clear the History folder of the viewed Web pages.

4 Save your changes, and exit the Options dialog box.

For more information about	See
Working with the History folder	Lesson 2
Saving a Web page to your computer	Lesson 2

Step 6: Search the Internet

You have never worked on an advertising campaign that buys radio air time. To learn more about radio stations in North America, you want to search for information on the Internet using Yahoo!

1   Display the available search engines.

2   Using Yahoo!, search for radio stations.

3   Select Business and Economy:Companies:Media:Radio Stations.

4   Click Western United States.

5   Review the list of radio stations in Salt Lake City, Utah, and then browse through one of the radio station Web sites.

For more information about	See
Finding information on the Internet	Lesson 3
Using key words to find a page	Lesson 3
Exploring search results	Lesson 3

Finish the Review & Practice

1   To continue to the next lesson, return to your Custom Start Page.

2   If you are finished using Internet Explorer for now, close the Internet Explorer window.

   If The Microsoft Network is your Internet service provider, the Microsoft Network dialog box appears.

   If you are using another Internet service provider's, you may be disconnected immediately.

3   If necessary, follow your service provider's instructions to disconnect from the network.

Communicating with Internet Users

Part 2

Using E-mail

In this lesson you will learn how to:

Estimated time
40 min.

- Use the Address Book, and address e-mail messages.
- Edit and send e-mail messages.
- Locate and read e-mail messages.
- Reply to and forward e-mail messages.
- Delete e-mail messages.
- Save and print e-mail messages.

It's easy to communicate information quickly to just about anyone who uses the Internet. When you want to give your co-worker some written information, you can print a memo and put it on her desk. If your co-worker is in another building, a branch office, or even another country, you can send the information to her via interoffice mail, regular mail, or overnight delivery. However, using the Internet, you can quickly send the memo as electronic mail, called *e-mail*, without leaving your computer. In addition, you can receive e-mail from your co-workers and friends directly on your computer.

Quick, economical, and easy to use, e-mail is fast becoming one of the most popular forms of communication between individuals around the world. Using e-mail, you can send a message to a friend in Russia and receive a reply the same day. When you receive the reply, you can read the message immediately or store it in your Inbox. After you've read the message, you can reply to it, store it in a folder within the program, print it, or delete it.

E-mail doesn't work through Internet browser programs such as Microsoft Internet Explorer; to use e-mail, you need to use a separate program specifically designed to send, receive, forward, and manage e-mail. There are numerous messaging systems on the market, including Microsoft Exchange, Eudora, and Pegasus. Microsoft's new e-mail program, Microsoft Internet Mail, comes with Internet Explorer and is specifically designed to handle e-mail over the Internet. In this lesson, you will learn how to send, receive, read, and store e-mail messages using Internet Mail.

WARNING If you are using Microsoft Exchange as your mail messaging program, do not install the Internet Mail component of Internet Explorer. Internet Mail will overwrite Exchange as your default mail program for all mail actions on your computer. To skip installing Internet Mail, click Yes when asked if you would like to select which optional Internet components are installed, click to remove the check mark from Internet Mail, and then click OK.

IMPORTANT Microsoft Internet Mail is an e-mail program specifically designed for use on the Internet. To send and receive e-mail, you must have a computer connected to a modem or a network and have Internet access. In addition, your Internet service provider must be able to support the standard Internet protocols—Simple Mail Transfer Protocol (SMTP) and Post Office Protocol (POP3). If you need to install Internet Mail, see Appendix B, "Setting Up Internet Mail, Internet News, and NetMeeting," for instructions.

If you are using The Microsoft Network as your Internet service provider, you cannot use Internet Mail as your messaging system because The Microsoft Network does not support SMTP and POP3 at this time. Instead, you will need to use Microsoft Exchange as your messaging system, which comes with Windows 95 and Windows NT. If you are using Microsoft Exchange as your Internet e-mail program, the basics of the program are given in the shaded boxes throughout this lesson. For more information about the program, see the *Microsoft Exchange Step by Step* book.

The Internet Explorer default e-mail program is Internet Mail; however, you can change the default to Microsoft Exchange. In the Internet Explorer window, on the View menu, click Options, and then click the Programs tab. Click the Mail down arrow, and select the e-mail program you want.

Setting the Scene

At Fitch & Mather, your advertising team has been working on the Amazing Mouse campaign. You have received several messages from two team members regarding the ad project. In this lesson, you'll learn how to quickly create and send new messages, respond to your messages, forward messages to additional recipients, save messages, and print messages, so that you can be prepared for a presentation with Fitch & Mather's clients.

Starting the Lesson

When you start Internet Mail, the Internet Mail window opens. In this window, you can send, receive, view, and organize your messages. When you first start the program, the Internet Mail toolbar appears at the top of the window. The toolbar displays menu shortcuts that help you work with your messages. The message list appears below the toolbar. The *message list* contains all the read and unread messages that you have received. The Preview Pane appears below the message list. The *Preview Pane* automatically displays the contents of each selected message so that you can quickly browse through your messages.

Start Internet Mail

The Internet

Mail

1 On the Desktop, double-click The Internet icon to open Internet Explorer. Maximize the window.

2 Click the Mail button, and then click Read Mail.

The Internet Mail window opens with the Inbox displayed.

Using the Address Book

To correct a typing error, press CTRL +Z, or on the Edit menu, click Undo and then continue typing.

One of the first things you'll want to do in Internet Mail is put entries in the Address Book. The Address Book is a quick and convenient way of storing e-mail addresses. Instead of typing the same addresses repeatedly, you can store the e-mail address in the Address Book. When you want to send an e-mail message, you open the Address Book and select the correct address. Internet Mail automatically enters the e-mail address in the To box.

Add practice e-mail addresses to your Address Book

1   On the File menu, click Address Book.

The Address Book window opens. It looks similar to the following illustration.

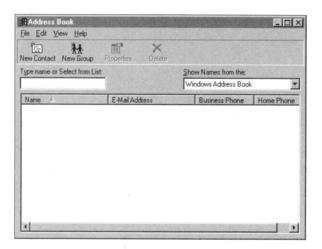

2   On the toolbar, click the New Contact button.

The Properties dialog box appears; the Personal tab is in front.

3   In the First box in the Name area, type **Beth** and then press the TAB key twice.

4   In the Last box in the Name area, type **Yamada** and then press TAB.

5   In the E-Mail Addresses box, type **bethy@www.fnm.com** and then click the Add button.

Beth Yamada's e-Mail address appears under E-mail Addresses in the second box.

6 Click OK.

The Properties dialog box closes. Beth Yamada's address is selected in the Address Book window.

7 On the toolbar, click the New Contact button.

The Properties dialog box appears.

8 In the First box in the Name area, type **Cathy** and then press TAB twice.

9 In the Last box in the Name area, type **Abdul** and then press TAB once.

10 In the E-Mail Addresses box, type **cathya@www.fnm.com** and then click Add.

Cathy Abdul's e-mail address appears under E-Mail Addresses in the second box.

11 Click OK.

The Properties dialog box closes, and Cathy Abdul's address is selected in the Address Book window. You now have two e-mail addresses in your Address Book that you can use throughout this lesson.

12 Close the Address Book window.

Creating and Addressing E-mail

When you want to send a message using Internet Mail, you begin by creating a new message. When you click the New Message button, a blank form is displayed, which serves as a template to help you compose your message and identify the recipients.

IMPORTANT To learn how to use e-mail, you should work with at least one other person. If possible, address your messages to a co-worker or friend throughout this lesson. Otherwise, follow the exercises in this lesson and address the messages to yourself.

Create a message

▶ On the toolbar, click the New Message button.

A new message form appears, and the insertion point is in the To box. Your screen should look similar to the following illustration.

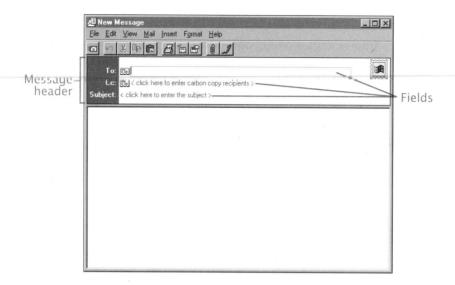

Message header — To: / Cc: / Subject: — Fields

You address your message by entering recipient names in the To area located at the top of the *message header*. This area is similar to that of a traditional memo where the recipients are identified at the top of the memo. In Internet Mail, you can type addresses or use the Address Book to identify recipients.

To select an e-mail recipient from your Address Book, click the index card beside To.

The form contains several boxes, or *fields*, that you fill in. Information is required in some boxes, such as the To box, but is optional in others, such as the Subject box. Although the Subject box is optional, typing a subject line helps recipients quickly identify the contents of your message. Good explanatory text in the Subject box can mean the difference between having your message read immediately or having it languish in the recipient's Inbox.

TIP You can add multiple recipients to the To box by typing the addresses and a semi-colon and a space between each address. Sometimes, however, you might want to send someone a copy of the message. This is called Cc, or carbon copying. To send someone a Cc, click Click Here To Enter Carbon Copy Recipients, and then type the recipient's e-mail address.

Address a message

In this exercise, you address a message to yourself and enter text in the Subject box. Although you would probably not normally send a message to yourself, this is an easy way to practice creating and sending a message. You can send your practice message to someone else if you'd rather.

For information on how to read Internet addresses, refer to Lesson 1, "Traveling the World Wide Web."

1 Type your e-mail address, and then press TAB twice.

The insertion point moves to the Subject box. Be sure to type your e-mail address exactly.

2 Type **Congratulations** and then press TAB.

The insertion point moves to the message area.

Entering Message Text

Now that you've addressed an e-mail message and typed a subject line, it's time to add the message text. As you type, Internet Mail automatically wraps the text to the next line for you. In addition, your message is not limited to a set number of lines. You can, for example, add several paragraphs to an e-mail message.

 TIP Using Internet Mail, you can have fun creating messages with different kinds of formatting using a special feature known as HTML formatting. You can create bulleted items, change type styles and sizes, add color, and even change the alignment of your text. To add formatting features to your text, in the New Message window, click HTML on the Format menu. The HTML toolbar appears below the message header but above the message area. As you type your message, use the toolbar to choose the formatting features that you want. Go ahead and have fun experimenting! When you send your message, if the recipients have software that can read HTML formatting, such as Internet Mail or Exchange, they can see your formatting. Otherwise, the message appears as plain text with an HTML file attached.

Enter the message text

 Type **Now I can communicate on the Internet.**

Sending Messages

Now that you've addressed and composed a message, you're ready to send it. When you send a message, regardless of whether you composed the message *online* (while connected to your Internet service provider or the Internet) or *offline* (while you're disconnected from your service provider or the Internet), the message moves first to the Outbox, where it is stored until you tell Internet Mail to deliver it. Storing your messages in the Outbox until you're ready to send them is a money-saving feature. You can create all your messages offline, store them in the Outbox, and then send all the messages when you go online.

It's not necessary for a recipient to be online when the message is received; the message is stored on the recipient's mail server or the service provider's server until the recipient logs on to the Internet. The *server* is the computer that handles incoming and outgoing messages. Finally, if your e-mail message cannot be delivered because of a network problem or an incorrect address, you'll receive a notification message telling you that the message is undeliverable.

Send a message

Why waste a perfectly good e-mail? Now that you've addressed and created a message, send it to yourself. In this exercise, you'll send your message to yourself, and then you'll view it.

Send

1 On the toolbar, click the Send button.

A message appears.

2 Click OK.

Your message is sent to the Outbox.

3 On the toolbar, click the Send And Receive button.

All the messages stored in your Outbox are sent to their respective recipients. In addition, Internet Mail moves any messages waiting for you into your Inbox.

 TIP You can change your Internet Mail options to have your e-mail messages transmitted when you click the Send button. On the Mail menu, click Options, and then select the Send Messages Immediately check box.

Creating E-mail Messages Using Microsoft Exchange

Microsoft Exchange works a little differently from Microsoft Internet Mail. If you want to use Exchange and haven't installed it yet, refer to Appendix A, "Setting Up Your Internet Connection." After you install Exchange, double-click the Inbox icon on your Desktop. The Microsoft Exchange Inbox appears.

To create and send a message in Exchange, click the New Message button. In the To box, type the e-mail address of the recipient. In the Subject box, type the subject of the message. Type your message in the message area. Click the Send button.

You can create an address in Exchange by clicking the Address Book button, and then the New Entry button. Select the e-mail type, for example, an Internet e-mail address or a MacMail address, and then select the location where you want to store the e-mail address. Click OK. In the Alias box, type the name of the person, and then in the SMTP box, type the e-mail address. Click OK. The address appears in your Address Book now.

Locating and Reading Messages

When you start Internet Mail, the main window opens. You can easily identify and manage your incoming messages in the Internet Mail window because they're automatically placed in the Inbox folder.

 TIP To be automatically notified when you get a message, click Options on the Mail menu, click the Read tab, and then select the Check For New Messages Every x Minutes check box. Click OK.

Viewing Folders to Locate Messages

By default, your Internet Mail window includes the following four built-in folders.

Inbox folder When you receive an incoming message in Internet Mail, an icon appears on the status bar, indicating that a new message has been delivered to your Inbox. You can also be notified by a chiming sound and the pointer changing briefly to a small message icon. All the messages sent to you from other people are delivered to your Inbox folder; these messages remain in the Inbox until you move or delete them.

Sent Items folder By default, a copy of each message you send is placed in your Sent Items folder, so it is not necessary to Cc yourself to retain a copy of the messages you send. All sent messages are stored in the Sent Items folder until you delete or move them.

Outbox folder The Outbox is the temporary storage area for outgoing messages until they are delivered.

Deleted Items folder Messages that you delete are moved to the Deleted Items folder. By default, deleted messages remain in this folder until you empty the folder. You can set up your options so that the Deleted Items folder is automatically emptied when you exit Internet Mail.

Later in this lesson, you will learn how to create additional folders and move messages from one folder to another.

You can easily distinguish between different messages in the message list by reading the message header. The message header identifies the sender, the subject, and the date and time the message was sent. Messages that have not been read are in bold type and a closed envelope icon is beside the header. Messages that have been opened are in regular type, and an opened envelope icon is beside the header.

Explore your mailbox folders

In this exercise, you open your built-in folders to view where different messages are stored. You can review the message you sent congratulating yourself and see if any messages are located in any other folders in your mailbox.

1   Click the Folders down arrow, and then click Deleted Items.

The Deleted Items message list should show no messages stored in the Deleted Items folder because you have not deleted any messages yet.

2   Click the Folders down arrow, and then click Outbox.

The Outbox folder message list should show no messages stored in the Outbox folder.

3   Click the Folders down arrow, and then click Sent Items.

The Sent Items folder message list should show the Congratulations message that you sent.

4   Click the Folders down arrow, and then click Inbox.

The Congratulations message and any other messages you received appear in the message list.

Creating Folders and Moving Messages Using Microsoft Exchange

To create folders in Microsoft Exchange, on the File menu, click New Folder. In the New Folder dialog box, type the name of the new folder. Click OK. The new folder appears in your Folder list.

The purpose of creating new folders is to move messages into them. To move messages in Exchange, select the messages you want to move, and then on the File menu, click Move. Select the folder you want to move the messages to, and then click OK. You can also drag a message to another folder.

Reading Messages

Each message you receive appears in the folder's message list. The message list displays the sender, the subject, and the date and time the message was sent.

 TIP   Using the Preview Pane, you can view your messages without opening them. Click the message you want to preview. The message appears in the Preview Pane.

Open a message

In this exercise, you open a message so that you can read it.

1   Double-click the Congratulations message so you can read it.

A copy of the message you sent opens. Your message should look similar to the following illustration.

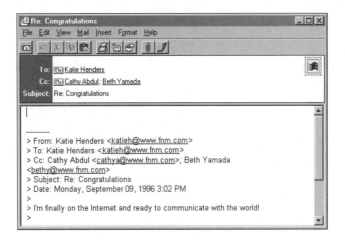

2   Close the Congratulations window.

Reading Your Messages Using Microsoft Exchange

When you receive a message in Microsoft Exchange, an icon in the shape of an addressed envelope appears on the status bar. In the Folder list, which is the left pane of the Exchange window, click the Inbox. In the right pane of the Inbox, the message list is displayed. New messages appear in bold and read messages appear in regular text. Like Internet Mail, Exchange displays High and Low priority icons, a paper clip icon to represent attachments, and envelope icons to represent messages. Columns separate the header information into priority, messages, attachments, the name of the sender, the subject text and the date and time received. To reorganize the messages by author or date received, click on the corresponding column title at the top of the message list.

To read a message, double-click on the message. The message appears in a separate window. Click the Next button to read the next message, or click the Previous button to read the previous message.

Replying to Messages

Sooner or later you'll want to reply to a message. When you do, you can create a new message, add the recipient and the subject, and then try to recall the details of the original message. But it's usually better if you and the recipient can see the original message along with your reply. It's much easier to keep track of your e-mail conversations that way. To include the original message with your response, you select or open the message and then use the Reply To Author feature.

Reply to a message

In this exercise, you reply to the message you sent yourself.

Reply to
Author

1   Select your Congratulations message.

2   On the toolbar, click the Reply To Author button.

    The Re: Congratulations window opens, and the original message appears with a > symbol at the beginning of every text line. To indicate that this message is in response to a previous message, Internet Mail automatically inserts a "Re:" before the Subject text.

3   In the Cc box, click the Address icon.

    The Select Recipients dialog box appears.

4   Click Beth Yamada's name, and then click the CC button. Click Cathy Abdul's name, and then click the CC button again.

5   Click OK.

Send

6   Click in the message window, and then type **I'm finally on the Internet and ready to communicate with the world!** Click the Send button.

7   Click OK.

8   On the toolbar, click the Send And Receive button if you haven't changed your settings to automatically send e-mail when you click the Send button.

Send and
Receive

    Your reply is sent to you, Beth Yamada, and Cathy Abdul.

9   Click the Folders down arrow, and then click Inbox.

 IMPORTANT   Before continuing, you need to receive your message. Wait a few moments and then click the Send And Receive button to collect your message. When the message arrives in your Inbox, continue with the exercises. Two additional messages appear in your Inbox. From Mail Administrator, these messages are automatically generated by the server to indicate that the messages you sent to Beth Yamada and Cathy Abdul cannot be delivered. You can delete the messages immediately, or you can delete them at the end of this lesson.

Replying to All

When you use the Reply To Author feature, you're responding only to the person who sent the message. But if you want to respond to all the recipients listed in the original message, you can use the Reply To All feature.

Reply to all

In this exercise, you reply to the Re: Congratulations message that you sent yourself, Beth Yamada, and Cathy Abdul.

1 Click the Re: Congratulations message.

You don't have to open a message to send a reply.

2 On the toolbar, click the Reply To All button.

The Re: Congratulations form appears with the To and Subject boxes filled, as shown in the following illustration. Notice that Beth Yamada and Cathy Abdul appear in the Cc box.

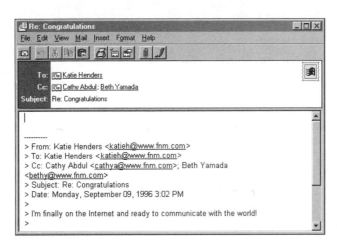

3 Type **If they have e-mail addresses, I'd like to send messages to my friends and family. I can easily keep in touch with everyone.**

4 Click Send.

The message window closes and the message is moved to the Outbox.

5 Click OK.

6 On the toolbar, click the Send And Receive button if you haven't changed your settings to automatically send e-mail when you click the Send button.

Your reply is sent to you, Beth Yamada, and Cathy Abdul.

> ### Replying To and Forwarding Messages Using Microsoft Exchange
>
> Using Microsoft Exchange, you can reply to the sender or to all the recipients of the message. To reply to an e-mail message, select the message in your Inbox and on the toolbar, click the Reply To Sender button. Type your message in the message area and then on the toolbar, click the Send button.
>
> If you want to reply to all the recipients of a message, select the message. On the toolbar, click the Reply To All button. Type your message and then click the Send button.
>
> When you want to forward a message to another recipient, select the message. On the toolbar, click the Forward button. Type the recipient's address and then type your message in the message area. Click the Send button.

Forwarding Messages

You can also forward a copy of a message to a new recipient, rather than retype or print out a copy of the message. You can forward a message to several people or add carbon copy recipients, just as you can in any other message. Keep in mind that just as you can forward messages that you receive from other people, others can forward any message you send, to whomever they want!

A forward message opens with a new message header and a blank message area. You must fill out the new message header; however, adding a message of your own is optional. The original message, including the original message header, is at the bottom. Forwarded messages are identified by the letters "Fw" in the subject area.

 IMPORTANT After you send the Re: Congratulations message to yourself, wait a few moments and then click the Send And Receive button again. The message should appear in your Inbox.

Forward a message

In this exercise, you forward the Re: Congratulations message to Henry D'Anconia.

1   Click the first Re: Congratulations message you sent yourself and Cc'd to Beth Yamada and Cathy Abdul.

    You don't have to open the message to send a reply.

2   On the toolbar, click the Forward button.

    The insertion point is in the To box.

3 Type **henryd@www.fnm.com** and then press the TAB key three times.

The insertion point is in the message area. Notice that Fw: Congratulations appears in the Subject box.

> **NOTE**   Internet Mail automatically creates links to e-mail and Web addresses when you type the address in your message. When you forward a message, you might see highlighted text in your message window. If you click a highlighted e-mail address, a New Message form appears with the e-mail address entered in the To box. Now you can create the message just like any other e-mail message. If you click a highlighted Web address, Internet Explorer opens and displays the Web page.

4 Type **I'm forwarding this message to you so that you know I've arrived on the Internet.**

Send

5 On the toolbar, click the Send button.

Your message is sent to the Outbox.

6 Click OK.

7 On the toolbar, click the Send And Receive button if you haven't changed your settings to automatically send e-mail when you click the Send button.

Browsing Through Messages

As you look in the Internet Mail window, you can see that icons appear to the left of the messages. Different kinds of messages are identified by different icons. For example, an attachment icon looks like a paper clip beside an envelope. To assign message priority, on the Mail menu in the New Message window, click Set Priority and then select High, Normal, or Low. Some of the different icons used to identify messages in the folder message list are listed in the following table.

Icon	Description
▣	Standard e-mail with normal priority
! ▣	E-mail with high priority
↓ ▣	E-mail with low priority
◌ ▣	E-mail with an attached file
✉	Read e-mail

In the message list, the priority icons appear on the far left; next is the read or unread icon, which is followed by the name of the sender, the subject, and the date and time. By default, messages are displayed in date order, with the most recent message at the top of the list.

 TIP You can display your messages in the message list in alphabetical order by recipient name, by subject, or by date received. To arrange messages by recipient name, click the From button above the messages. To arrange the messages by subject, click the Subject button.

There are now several practice messages in your Inbox. Because you have not read these messages, they are in bold type. Now that you know how to open a message, you can read all your new messages. When you open a message that is a reply or a forwarded message, the original message text is included at the bottom of the message by default.

Browse through messages

In this exercise, you browse through your messages.

1   Click the Folders down arrow, and then click Inbox.

Your message list changes to display all the messages that you have received.

2   Double-click the Congratulations message.

The message opens.

3   On the toolbar, click the Next button until the message Re: Congratulations appears.

4   Read the message.

5   On the toolbar, click the Previous button.

The Congratulations message that you sent appears in the window.

6   Close the Congratulations window.

Next

Previous

Deleting Messages

After you've finished reading and responding to a message, you should decide whether you want to save it. If you save all the messages you receive, they'll occupy a lot of storage space and they'll be hard to organize. If you don't need a message any longer, then you should delete it.

Deleted messages are moved to the Deleted Items folder, so if you change your mind about deleting a message, you can still retrieve it. The Internet Mail default is set up to store the deleted messages in the Deleted Items folder until you open the folder and delete each item. Any messages you delete from the Deleted Items folder are permanently removed from your computer system.

 TIP You can print copies of your messages. Click the message you want to print, and then on the File menu, click Print. Click the Name down arrow, and then click the name of your printer. Under Print Range, select the pages that you want to print. Under Copies, use the Number Of Copies arrows to select the number of copies that you want to print. Click OK.

Delete a message

In this exercise, you delete the messages from your Inbox.

 IMPORTANT Make sure you delete only the practice messages and not any real messages you might have.

1 Click the Congratulations message that you sent yourself.

2 On the toolbar, click the Delete button.

The message is removed from your message list.

To select several nonconsecutive messages, hold down the ALT key while you click the messages you want.

 TIP If you decide to keep messages that you've received, you should organize them so that they don't clutter your Inbox. To organize your messages, you can create folders in Internet Mail and then move the messages to the appropriate folder. On the File menu, click Folder and then Create. Type a file folder name and then click OK. Select the messages you want to move into the folder. On the Mail menu, click Move To and then the file folder name. The messages are moved into the new folder.

View the Deleted Items folder

1 Click the Folders down arrow, and then click Deleted Items.

The contents of the Deleted Items folder, including your Congratulations message, appear in the Internet Mail window.

2 Click your Congratulations message, and then click the Delete button.

A message asks if you're sure you want to permanently delete the message.

TIP If you want Internet Mail to delete all messages from the Deleted Items folder whenever you exit the program, you can change your default settings. In the main Internet Mail window, click Options on the Mail menu. Click the Read tab, and then select the Empty Messages From The Deleted Items Folder On Exit check box. Click OK.

3 Click Yes.

Your Congratulations message is permanently removed from the Deleted Items folder.

4 Click the Folders down arrow, and then click Inbox.

The Inbox opens.

Deleting a Message Using Microsoft Exchange

In your Inbox, select the message you want to delete. On the toolbar, click the Delete button. By default, the Deleted Items folder is automatically emptied when you close Microsoft Exchange.

One Step Further: Attaching a File to an E-mail Message

Attaching files to messages is helpful when you already have a file created and want the recipients to easily copy it to their hard disk. If your recipients have the program that was used to create an attached file, or if they have a program that recognizes the file type, they can open and edit the file on their computer. To open an attached file, you double-click the icon in the message.

You can also attach a file as a text-only file, although no text formatting will be retained. This is especially useful if the text you want to send is heavily formatted and the recipient's e-mail program cannot read formatted text files. This can occur when you send files over the Internet or to non–Microsoft Internet Mail server mail systems.

Attach a file

In this exercise, you'll attach the aweinfo file to a message to Cathy Abdul.

1 On the toolbar, click the New Message button.

2   In the To box, type **cathya@www.pbt.com** and then press the TAB key twice.

3   In the Subject box, type **Awesome Computers info,** and then press TAB.

4   Type **I'm attaching a file with Awesome Computers data. Please review and then we can discuss it on Thursday.** Press ENTER.

5   On the toolbar, click the Insert File button.

Insert File

To send a file as text-only, click the Text Only option under Insert As.

6   Verify that the IE 3.0 SBS Practice folder is open on your CD-ROM drive.

7   Click the aweinfo file.

8   Click Attach.

The attached file appears as an icon, as shown in the following illustration.

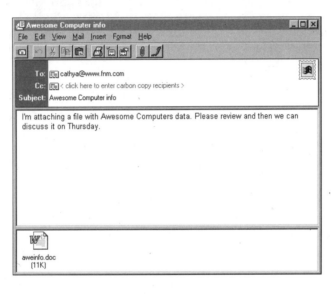

Send

9   Click the Send button, and then click OK.

10   Click the Send And Receive button.

Your reply, with the attached file, is sent.

When you send an encoded or compressed file, make sure you indicate the compressed or encoded file format.

Encoding or Compressing Files

If you attach a file to a message, the message is usually too big for most e-mail systems to handle. In that case, the message could be returned to you as undeliverable, or, if the recipient gets the message, it could be unreadable. A way to get around this problem is to encode the message. When you *encode* a message, Internet Mail chops the message up into smaller pieces so that the file can be easily transmitted. Each piece is sent to the recipient, whose e-mail program reassembles the message when it is delivered. Neither you nor your recipient has to fuss with any technical stuff. Your e-mail program and the recipient's e-mail program do it all.

To automatically encode attached messages, click Options on the Mail menu. Click the Send tab, select the Break Apart Messages Larger Than KB check box, and use the arrows to select a size. Under the Mail Sending Format, click the Settings button. Choose the encoding type (MIME or Uuencode), and then click OK. The MIME (Multipurpose Internet Mail Extension) encoding format is the most commonly used format, so try using MIME first and, if that doesn't work, then use Uuencode.

Besides encoded files, you'll probably encounter compressed files. A *compressed file* is comprised of one or more files that have been squished. Imagine a loaf of bread. When you squeeze both ends of the bread toward the middle, the bread becomes smaller. All the slices of bread are still there, they just occupy less space. Compressed files work in the same fashion except that, unlike bread, compressed files can be decompressed. To compress and decompress files, you need a special program, such as WinZip for compressing and decompressing files, or Pkzip for compressing files and PKUnzip for decompressing files. There are plenty of shareware programs available on the Web for compressing and decompressing files. See Lesson 1, "Travelling the World Wide Web," for information on downloading.

Finish the lesson

Follow these steps to delete the practice messages you created in this lesson.

 NOTE If you have your own messages in the Inbox, be sure you delete only the practice files and messages you added or created during this lesson.

1   In your Inbox folder and Sent Items folder, select the practice messages that you used in this lesson, and press DELETE.

2 Close the Microsoft Internet Mail window.

3 If you want to continue to the next lesson, double-click the Internet News icon.

You are logged on to Microsoft Internet News.

Lesson Summary

To	Do this	Button
Start Internet Mail	In Internet Explorer, click the Internet Mail button, and then click Read Mail.	
Create a message	On the toolbar, click the New Message button.	New Message
Address a message	In the To box, type the full e-mail address.	
Send a message	On the toolbar, click the Send button.	
Enter and edit message text	In the message area, type your text. To edit, on the Edit menu, click Undo.	
View the contents of a folder	Click the folder in the message list.	
Open a message	Double-click the message. *or* Use the right mouse button to click the message, and then click Open.	
Browse to the next message	Open a message. On the toolbar, click the Next button.	
Browse to the previous message	Open a message. On the toolbar, click the Previous button.	
Create a folder	On the File menu, click Folder, and then click New. Type a name, and click OK.	
Reply to the author of a message	Click or open the message. On the toolbar, click the Reply To Author button.	Reply to Author
Reply to all	Click or open the message. On the toolbar, click the Reply To All button.	Reply to All

99

To	Do this	Button
Forward a message	Click or open the message. On the toolbar, click the Forward button.	Forward
Delete a message	Click or open the message. On the toolbar, click the Delete button or press the DELETE key.	Delete

For online information about	On the Help menu, click Help Topics. In the Help Topics dialog box, click Index, and then type
Using the Address Book	Address Book *or* addressing messages
Sending messages	sending messages
Viewing items in your Inbox	opening messages
Working with incoming messages	message folders *or* message headers
Replying to messages	replying to messages
Forwarding messages	forwarding messages
Sorting messages	sorting messages
Creating folders	folders adding

Communicating Through Newsgroups

Estimated time
30 min.

In this lesson you will learn how to:

- Set up your computer so that you can view newsgroups.
- Locate the newsgroup you want to view.
- Browse various newsgroups.
- Send an article to a newsgroup.

Have you ever had a question that you wanted to ask, but you didn't know who would have the answer? Have you ever tried to sell something, but your newspaper ads never seemed to reach the right audience? The solution to these problems might be newsgroups. *Newsgroups* are a collection of messages called *postings* or *articles* available to anyone who has access to a computer that has newsgroup reading capability. Newsgroups are one of the most popular features of the Internet. In newsgroups, you can communicate with other people about a variety of subjects. There are over 15,000 newsgroups. Any topic you want to talk to someone about is probably already covered by a newsgroup, and if it isn't, you can start a newsgroup specifically for that topic. Participating in a newsgroup, you can post notices or talk about subjects ranging from gardening, to computers, to new recipe ideas, to architecture, to how to build sand castles.

Understanding Newsgroups

Suppose you want to start carpooling to work, but you don't know whether any of your co-workers live near you. You can ask around the office, but it's a lot easier to put or *post* a message on the bulletin board in your company's lunch room. You post the message on the bulletin board, and your co-workers, at their leisure, read and respond to your message. Newsgroups on the Internet work the same way: you send a message to a newsgroup, and other users can read and respond to your message at their own convenience. An important difference is that instead of being limited to a number of readers in a specific location, your message can be read by thousands of people located around the world.

Anyone who reads an article can respond to it. This response can create a thread of newsgroup conversation. A *thread* is an article that has at least one reply to it. Some threads can be lengthy, having hundreds and hundreds of replies.

Most newsgroups are part of Usenet. *Usenet* (which is short for user network) is made up of thousands of computers connected to each other, as is the Internet. Usenet computers share newsgroup articles from millions of people around the world. Initially, Usenet was meant to be a place to post notices and news, but those using Usenet transformed it into a combination posting area and chat room.

 NOTE Newsgroups have evolved into something similar to a *chat room*, where people converse back and forth. However, a chat room features "live" conversations through typewritten messages. You type a comment, and then the person you are chatting with can answer by typing a reply immediately. Newsgroups are not "live" discussion areas and have much slower response times than a discussion in a chat room.

When you post an article, it is stored in your geographical area on a computer, called a *news server*, which is simply a computer dedicated to the storage of newsgroups. There are thousands of news servers all over the world. News servers are connected to each other, just as the various computers of the Internet are connected to each other.

How Do Newsgroups Stay Current?

Every day, your local Usenet news server transfers or copies your article and any other new articles stored on its hard disk to other news servers, which in turn pass on their own new postings and your server's new postings to other servers, like a giant chain letter. Eventually, the postings are available on all the Usenet servers in the world.

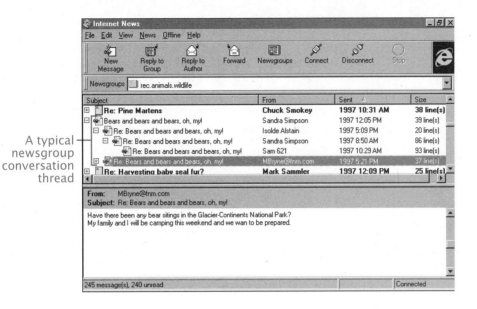

A typical newsgroup conversation thread

Start Internet Explorer

> **IMPORTANT** To successfully complete this lesson, you will need to have a computer, a modem, and a dial-up connection to an Internet service provider or a connection to the Internet through a network. In addition, you must have Internet Explorer 3.0 installed.

The Internet

If you are connected to the Internet through a network connection, skip step 2 through step 4.

1 On the Desktop, double-click The Internet icon.

The Internet Explorer window opens, and The Microsoft Network Sign In dialog box appears. If you have not installed The Microsoft Network, a dialog box appears asking if you want to install the program.

2 In the Member ID box, type your Member ID.

This is the name you gave yourself when you set up The Microsoft Network.

3 In the Password box, type your password.

If you don't want to type your password every time you connect to The Microsoft Network, click the Remember My Password check box. Use caution if you choose this option, because then anyone using MSN on your computer can gain access to your MSN account.

4 Click Connect.

Modem icon

After a few moments, The Microsoft Network window and the MSN To-day window open. If you are using a modem, on the taskbar, you will see a small modem icon in the status box.

103

*If you have
forgotten your
password, you
can call the MSN
Member Support
Center at
1-800-386-5550.*

TROUBLESHOOTING   If you cannot connect to The Microsoft Network, try the following: check your modem settings, verify that your modem is turned on (if it is an external modem) and connected to a phone jack, and check that you are using the correct phone number.

5   Verify that the Internet Explorer window is maximized.

If the Internet Explorer window is not maximized, click the Maximize button. After a few moments, a page on the World Wide Web appears.

Open Internet News

IMPORTANT   If you have not set up Internet News, go to Appendix B, "Setting Up Internet Mail, Internet News, and NetMeeting."

1   On the toolbar, click the Mail button, and then click Read News.

The Internet News window opens.

2   Maximize the Internet News window.

The window should look like the following illustration.

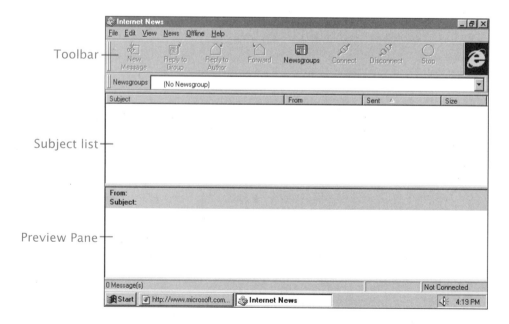

104

Connecting to Newsgroups

The thousands of newsgroups on Usenet contain articles that deal with a variety of subjects, from the mundane to the risqué. Typically, the name of a newsgroup describes the subject discussed in the newsgroup. Newsgroups are divided into different major categories, similar to the divisions of the want ads of a newspaper. The first part of a newsgroup name is the abbreviation of the newsgroup category, followed by a period, and then more descriptive words to narrow the topic. For example, biz.comp.hardware is the name of a newsgroup in the category of business, that has a subject of computer hardware. The main newsgroup top-level categories and their abbreviations are described in the table below.

Category name	Abbreviation	Includes
Alternative	alt	Topics covering any possible interest. If a topic doesn't fit into any other newsgroup, it goes here. Includes professional sports, recipes, fan clubs, discussion about computer languages, and politics.
Business	biz	Business-related topics. Includes information about computer services, discussions of the marketplace, and general business topics.
Computers	comp	Topics of interest to computer users, both professionals and hobbyists. Includes information about software, hardware, and computer science.
General news	news	Discussions of Usenet itself. Includes software, maintenance, new newsgroups, and statistics.
Recreational	rec	Topics relating to hobbies and recreational activities. Includes movies, sports, hobbies, and travel.
Scientific	sci	Knowledgeable discussions relating to established sciences, research, and applications. Includes physics, astronomy, and medical research.
Social	soc	Addresses social and cultural issues. Includes religion, language, and ethnicity.

Category name	Abbreviation	Includes
Debate-oriented	talk	Debates on controversial topics. Includes abortion, religion, and guns
Miscellaneous newsgroups	misc	Topics not easily classified into other categories, or containing themes from more than one newsgroup category. Includes information about kids, investing, law, and employment.

Viewing Newsgroups

The first step to finding an article on a subject is to view the list of newsgroups on your server. There can be thousands of newsgroups on a news server; the groups are listed in alphabetical order by category.

View newsgroups

In this exercise, you view the newsgroups on your news server.

➤ On the toolbar, click the Newsgroups button.

The Newsgroups window opens and contains a list of newsgroups. The dialog box should look similar to the following illustration.

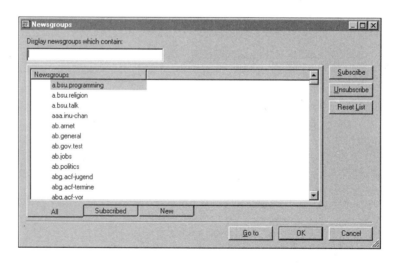

Finding a Newsgroup

Because there are thousands of newsgroups on a server, it can be tedious or difficult to search through all the different newsgroups for one about your subject. To help you find the newsgroup you are looking for, Internet News has a feature that will search for a subject you want to find. The search feature scans the list of newsgroups on your news server and finds the newsgroups that have the words you want to read about. You do not have to use the search feature to select a newsgroup. You can also scroll through the list and select newsgroups.

Search for a newsgroup

You are interested in finding general information about newsgroups, so you decide to search for a newsgroup that contains information for the new newsgroup user. In this exercise, you search for news newsgroups.

1 Make sure the insertion point is in the Display Newsgroups Which Contain box.

2 In the Display Newsgroups Which Contain box, type **news**

All the newsgroups disappear from the list except those that contain the letters "news."

3 Type **.newusers**

Only the news.newusers.questions newsgroup remains because it is the only one that contains the search words you typed.

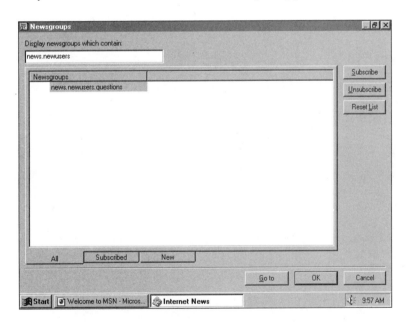

Subscribing to a Newsgroup

When you find a newsgroup that sounds interesting, you have to select the newsgroup before you can view the articles contained in it. During your search of Usenet newsgroups, you will come across some newsgroup that you want to return to again and again. The fastest way to repeatedly open a newsgroup is to *subscribe* to the newsgroup. Subscribing to a newsgroup is similar to subscribing to a magazine, but you don't have to pay to subscribe to a newsgroup. After you have subscribed to a newsgroup, it is included in your list of newsgroups in the Internet News window so you don't have to open the Newsgroup window. After you have selected a newsgroup, you can open the newsgroup and view the articles you want.

 NOTE If you no longer want to subscribe to a newsgroup, for whatever reason, you can unsubscribe from the newsgroup. Simply click the Newsgroup button on the toolbar, select the newsgroup you want to cancel your subscription to, and then click the Unsubscribe button.

In these exercises, you subscribe to the news.newusers.questions newsgroup. Then, you restore the display so that you can see the complete newsgroups listing again.

Subscribe to a newsgroup

1   In the Newsgroup box, be sure that news.newusers.questions is selected.

The news.newusers.questions newsgroup is selected.

You can also double-click the news.newusers. questions name.

2   Click the Subscribe button.

A small newspaper icon appears next to the news.newusers.questions newsgroup.

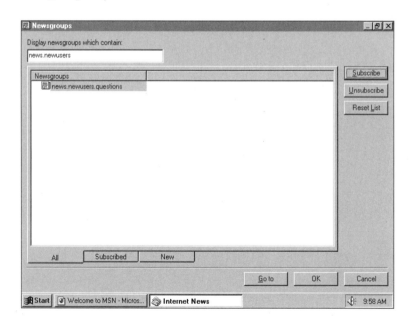

Clear the display to show all newsgroups

➤ In the Display Newsgroups Which Contain box, select the text, and then press DELETE.

The entire list of newsgroups is displayed.

Reading Messages in Newsgroups

Before you begin posting to a newsgroup, it's a good idea to spend some time doing what is known as "lurking." When you *lurk*, you read the messages in the newsgroup, but don't actively participate in the conversation. Lurking is a good idea at first because each newsgroup has its own tone and some groups use jargon specific to that newsgroup. Lurking helps you avoid mistakes that could accidentally start a written argument called a *flame war*. Look at how the newsgroup members talk to each other. This will give you an idea of the tone of the writing in the articles that are posted.

 TIP You can organize newsgroup articles by subject, by sender, by date, or by size. Click the subject column heading to sort the messages by subject, the sender column heading to sort the messages by sender, and so on.

Reading Articles

You can read any articles in any newsgroup on your news server. This is a great way to learn about a variety of subjects you know little or nothing about, or to learn more about subjects you know well. When you select an article to read, you see a preview of the article in the lower half of your Internet Explorer window. If you double-click the article, it opens in its own window.

When you use Internet News to view the newsgroups on your server, there are various icons next to the articles in the newsgroup. These icons show the status of the article that you want to view. Each icon, its name, and its meaning are shown in the following table.

Icon	Name	Description
⊞	Plus icon	Threaded conversation that is collapsed. Only the main article is shown, while all of the conversations threaded with it are hidden.
⊟	Minus icon	Threaded conversation that is expanded (that is, all the subarticles are displayed).
📄	Message and thumb tack icon	Read article whose title and message are stored on your computer.

109

Icon	Name	Description
▯	Plain message icon	Read article whose title is stored on your computer.
▤	Yellow message and thumb tack icon	Unread article whose title and message are stored on your computer.
▯	Yellow plain message icon	Unread article whose title is stored on your computer.

You want to read some articles and postings in the news.newusers.questions newsgroup to learn about using newsgroups. In these exercises, you open the news.newusers.questions newsgroup and then read some articles.

Open the news.newusers.questions newsgroup

1 Click Subscribe. Be sure that the news.newusers.questions newsgroup is selected.

A newsgroup must be selected before you can open it. If it is not selected, click to select it.

2 Click the Go To button.

The Newsgroup dialog box closes, and in the lower-left corner of the Internet News status bar a message appears, saying that Internet News is checking for new messages. After a moment, the titles, or *headers*, of the articles in the newsgroup are copied, or *downloaded*, to your machine. The articles in the news.newusers.questions newsgroup appear in a list.

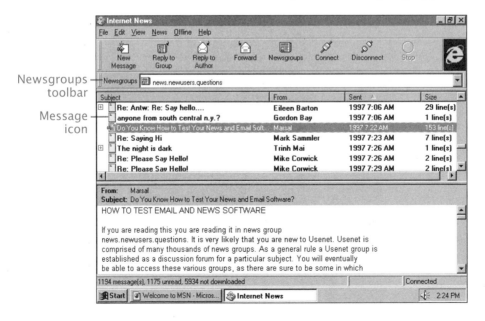

NOTE   Because newsgroups are constantly changing, in this exercise you will open any article you choose.

Read articles

1   Click an article in the news.newusers.questions newsgroup that looks interesting.

The article appears in the Preview Pane. The icon next to the articles changes to a piece of paper that has a thumb tack through it, the message icon. This icon and the regular, not bold, type indicate that the message has been read.

You can also click the article, and then press ENTER.

2   Double-click the article.

A new windows opens; the article is displayed in the window.

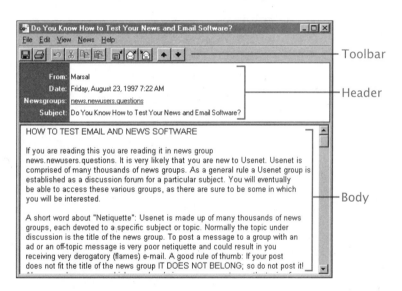

3   Close the article window.

Reading Related Messages and Responses

Threads of conversation are also grouped together in newsgroups. A message that is part of a thread has a plus symbol (+) next to it. Internet News shows the original message in the threaded message group, and hides the other later postings below the original article. When you click the plus symbol, a list of related articles or subarticles opens underneath the original message. Subarticles can also have their own threads of conversation, so there can be several layers of threads from one single, beginning article.

When you are following the thread of a conversation, you usually want to read one message after another. However, it is tedious to open a message, close the message, open another message, close that message, and so on. You can more quickly maneuver through messages using the Previous button and the Next button.

You decide to view a thread of conversation in the news.newusers.questions newsgroup. In these exercises, you'll expand a thread of conversation, and then follow the thread.

Expand a thread

➤ Find an article with a plus (+) sign, and click the plus sign.

The list of subarticles threaded to the article appears.

Follow a thread

1 Double-click the main article.

The article window opens.

2 On the article's toolbar, click the Previous button.

The article above opens.

3 On the article's toolbar, click the Next button.

The main article opens again.

4 Click the Next button.

The first response to that article opens.

Previous
You can also press CTRL <.

Next
You can also press CTRL >.

Printing or Saving Messages

If you come across an interesting article, you might want to print the article or save it to your hard disk. Typically, when you quit Internet News, all the newsgroup articles you've read are deleted from your view of the newsgroup list of articles. This keeps the newsgroup clean of already read articles. If you come across an article that you want to keep, but you don't want a printout of it, you can save the article, either by placing it in the Saved Items folder in Internet News or by saving it as a file on your hard disk. When you save an article in the Saved Items folder, the article is still located on the news reader, but instead of being automatically deleted when Internet News closes, the article is retained until you delete it from the folder.

You decide you would like to share the information in an article with some other co-workers. In these exercises, you decide to print the article, and then save a copy in your Saved Items folder. Then you change your mind and decide to store the article on your desktop.

Print an article

IMPORTANT You must have a printer installed on your computer to do the "Print an article" exercise. If you do not have a printer installed, skip to the "Save an article to your Saved Items folder" exercise.

➤ On the article's toolbar, click the Print button.

The article is printed.

You can also click Print on the File menu, or press CTRL+P.

Save an article to your Saved Items folder

1 On the File menu, click Save Message.

The Saved Message dialog box appears, stating that the article is saved.

2 Click OK.

3 Close the article window.

4 Click the Newsgroup down arrow, and then click Saved Items.

The article is stored in this folder.

Delete an article from a folder

1 In the Saved Items folder, click the article.

The article is selected.

You can also press CTRL+D.

2 On the File menu, click Delete.

An "X" appears through the icon next to the article. This indicates that the article has been deleted.

3 Click the Newsgroups down arrow, and select news.newusers.questions.

The news.newusers.questions newsgroup appears. When you return to the Saved Items folder, the article will not be in it.

Save an article to your Desktop

1 Double-click an article in the news.newusers.questions newsgroup.

The article window opens.

2 On the File menu, click Save As.

The Save Message As dialog box appears.

3 Click the Save In down arrow, and then click Desktop.

The Folder view changes to the Desktop. You can save a newsgroup article in any folder on your computer.

To open the file, double-click The Article icon on the Desktop.

4 Make sure the name of the article appears in the File Name box.

You can use a different file name by selecting the name in the File Name box and typing a new name.

5 Click Save.

The article is saved to your Desktop.

6 Close the article window.

Sending Articles to Newsgroups

After you have lurked in a newsgroup for a while, the desire to respond to some messages will probably be pretty strong. Then you will be part of the thread of the conversation in that newsgroup, and your opinion will be part of the discussion. But before you post your first article to a newsgroup, it is good to know the basic lay of the land.

 TIP Messages can get lengthy if all the respondents include the original messages they are responding to. To reduce the length of a message, you can change the Include Original Message In Reply Option. On the News menu, click Options, click the Send tab, and then clear the Include Original Message In Reply check box. The original message will not appear in the message window when you select either the Reply To Group or the Reply To Author buttons.

Learning Basic Internet Etiquette

Internet Etiquette, or *netiquette*, is an important part of using Usenet. Usenet does not have a central control agency that guides the content of newsgroups, but unspoken rules have formed between the users of Usenet. What is interesting about these rules is that they vary from newsgroup to newsgroup. What is acceptable in one newsgroup might be considered rude or inappropriate in another newsgroup. That is why it is a good idea to look through the articles, or lurk, before you participate in a newsgroup.

Some netiquette rules are, however, common to most newsgroups. If you use these rules as your guidelines, you will have less chance of offending someone or receiving an insulting response. The following table describes some things to keep in mind when using newsgroups.

Things to remember	Why
Don't use all uppercase letters.	TEXT IN UPPERCASE LETTERS IS CONSIDERED YELLING. Capitalize words sparingly for emphasis.
Be descriptive but brief.	There are thousands of articles available, and if you want yours to be read, you must make it intriguing enough and short enough to provoke interest.
Subjects should be short and descriptive.	Short subjects make wading through newsgroup articles easier.
Don't post meaningless articles.	Articles that just say "I agree" or "I disagree" are a waste of time and energy.
Be careful what you say.	Your ironic or humorous intent might not come across to the reader. You can use emoticons (see below for details) to help convey your meaning.
Never forget that you are communicating with other people.	Be careful that you do not insult or criticize other Usenet readers.
Look before you leap.	Read several articles in a newsgroup before you respond or add to the newsgroup. That way you will know the tone and atmosphere that the other readers use, and you will be able to blend in well.
Don't post the same article more than once.	This practice is called "spamming," and newsgroup readers really hate it.

If you are considerate and conscientious in your articles, you should have no problems interacting with your fellow Usenet users.

How Can I Express Myself in Newsgroup Articles?

Anytime you write a message, you might say something that can be misinterpreted by a reader. For example, your joke might be interpreted as a serious statement. A way to clarify your intentions to the reader is to use emoticons and acronyms. *Emoticons*, sometimes called *smileys*, are keyboard symbols that, when combined, create small, sideways faces that convey an emotion.

There is no rule as to when or which emoticon you should use in a given situation. Just be sure not to use them too often, because they can become annoying to the reader after a while. The following table describes a few of the most popular emoticons.

Emoticon	Keystrokes	Meaning
:-)	colon, dash, close parenthesis	You're smiling at a joke.
:-D	colon, dash, capital D	You think something is very funny.
;-)	semi-colon, dash, close parenthesis	You are winking.
:-/	colon, dash, front slash	You are scowling.
:-O	colon, dash, capital O	You are surprised.
>:-(	greater than, colon, dash, open parenthesis	You are angry.
:'-(	colon, apostrophe, dash, open parenthesis	You are crying.
:-(	colon, dash, open parenthesis	You are unhappy.
8^]	eight key, carat, close bracket	You are feeling over whelmed.
;-}	semi-colon, dash, close brace	You are wryly winking.
:-p	colon, dash, lowercase p	You are sticking your tongue out.
>:-)	greater than, colon, dash, close parenthesis	You have made a devilish remark.
O:-)	capital O, colon, dash, close parenthesis	You have made an innocent remark.
<:-)	less than, colon, dash, close parenthesis	You have asked what you believe to be a stupid question.

Acronyms are abbreviations of phrases. For example, NASA stands for the National Aeronautics and Space Administration. Newsgroup writers frequently use acronyms to abbreviate standard phrases. The following table describes some of the most common acronyms.

Acronym	Meaning
<BG>, <G>	Big grin
<g>	Grin
AFAIK	As far as I know
BTW	By the way
HTH	Hope this helps
IMHO	In my humble opinion
IMNSHO	In my not so humble opinion
IMO	In my opinion
IOW	In other words
LOL	Laughing out loud
OIC	Oh, I see
ROTFL	Rolling on the floor, laughing
RTFM	Read the "Fine" (ahem) Manual
YMMV	Your mileage may vary

Replying to Messages in Newsgroups

After you have lurked in a newsgroup for a while and familiarized yourself with basic Internet etiquette, you will probably want to respond to other people's messages, and even create and send your own. Suppose someone posts a message on a business newsgroup requesting information about how to set up a home business. Recently you read a helpful book on how to establish a small business out of your home, and now you want to tell the person who requested small business information about this book. You can post a response to the original message on the newsgroup so that all newsgroup readers can view your response in the thread, or you can respond privately so that only the person who posted the message can read your response. In general, unless most of the newsgroup members can benefit from your information, limit responses to private messages.

NOTE Sometimes you want to discuss an article directly with its author. You can use the Internet News Reply To Author feature to reply only to the author of a message. This sends an e-mail to the author of the article. For more information about e-mail, see Lesson 1, "Using E-mail."

Open a newsgroup

1   On the toolbar, click the Newsgroups button.

The Newsgroups dialog box appears.

2   In the Display Newsgroups Which Contain box, type **alt.test**

The newsgroups that contain the words alt.test appear in the list below.

3   Click alt.test, and then click Go To.

The articles in alt.test newsgroup appear.

Reply to a newsgroup

You have decided that newsgroups look really interesting, but want to practice before you start responding to articles in a established newsgroup, so you decide to test your skills first. In this exercise, you post a response to an article in the test newsgroup for all readers to read.

1   Click an article in the alt.test newsgroup.

The article is selected.

2   Click the Reply To Group button.

A window opens. On the title bar, Re: appears before the title of the article you are replying to. This indicates that you are responding to the message. The outgoing message window is divided into two panes. The top pane contains the Newsgroups and Subject information for your response. The Newsgroups box lists the newsgroups your response will be sent to and the Subject box indicates the subject of the message response. The text in the Subject box appears in the newsgroup as your subject heading. The bottom pane contains the outgoing message and the original message to which you are responding. The insertion point is in the message pane.

118

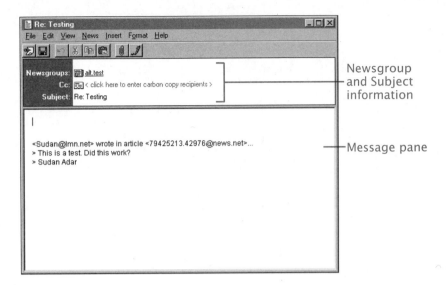

Newsgroup and Subject information

Message pane

3 In the message window, type **This is a test response. Please ignore.**

4 On the toolbar, click the Post Message button, and then click OK.

Your message is usually posted in the newsgroup within a few hours of being sent.

Post Message

 TIP You can add more newsgroups as recipients of your message. On the News menu, click Newsgroups. Select the name of the newsgroup that you want to add. Click Subscribe. The newsgroup name appears in the Newsgroups To Post To list. When you have finished adding newsgroups, click OK. The names of the newsgroups that will receive your message are in the Newsgroups list of the outgoing message.

Creating a New Newsgroup Message

Often you will have questions or information that you will post as a new article in a newsgroup. This is the great benefit of newsgroups. Within a day, your question or information can be viewed by thousands of people, and you can get quick results. The length of time it takes for an article to appear in a newsgroup depends on the number of times your Internet service provider news server updates the list of articles in each newsgroup. Create a new message

---

NOTE Sometimes when you post test messages to a test newsgroup, you will receive e-mail from other readers acknowledging that your test worked.

Create a new message

Now that you have responded to a message that was in the alt.test newsgroup, you have decided that you are ready to post your own message. In this exercise, you post a message.

New
Message

1   On the toolbar, click the New Message button.

The New Message window is similar to the illustration below. The name of the newsgroup to which you will post your message appears in the Newsgroup box.

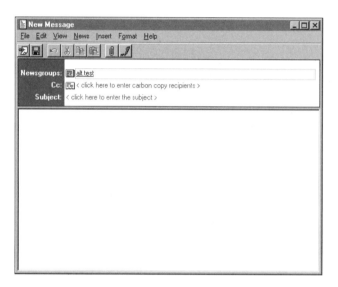

2   In the Newsgroups box, verify that alt.test appears, and then press TAB twice.

The insertion point moves to the Subject box.

 TIP   When you click the Reply to Group, Reply to Author, or the New Message icon, the newsgroup currently displayed in the Internet News window appears in the Newsgroups box. If you do not want to send your message to the current newsgroup, click the Newsgroups box and type the name of the newsgroup that you want to view.

3   In the Subject box, type **Testing – please ignore** and then press TAB.

4   In the message window, type **This is a test of how to post a message.**

Post Message

5 On the toolbar, click the Post Message button.

6 Click OK.

The message is posted to the newsgroup.

 NOTE If you'd like to build on the skills that you learned in this lesson, you can do the One Step Further. Otherwise, skip to "Finish the lesson."

One Step Further: Adding a News Server

During your use of newsgroups, you may find other news servers that contain information that your Internet service provider's news server doesn't offer. If you want to look at another news server, you can easily add another one to your list.

Add a news server

You have heard about a news server that Microsoft uses to post information about their products. You have the news server address and decide to add that news server to your list of servers.

1 On the News menu, click Options.

The Options dialog box appears. You use the Options dialog box to change the settings for your newsgroup viewing and posting.

2 Click the Server tab.

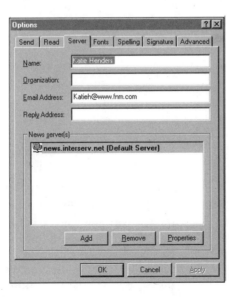

3 Click Add.

The News Server Properties dialog box appears.

4 In the News Server Name, type **msnews.microsoft.com** and click OK.

A message appears, asking if you would like to subscribe to the newsgroups available at msnews.microsoft.com.

5 Click Yes.

The Microsoft newsgroups appear in the Newsgroup dialog box, and the newsgroups are downloaded.

 NOTE To change to another news server, in the News Server column, click to select the icon of the news server you want to change to and select newsgroups from it.

---

6 Click OK, and then click OK again.

Finish the lesson

1 If you are finished using Internet News, click the Close button.

Internet News is not used in Lesson 6.

2 If you are finished using Internet Explorer for now, click the Close button on the Internet Explorer window.

The Microsoft Network dialog box appears.

3 Click Yes.

Your modem is disconnected, and Internet Explorer closes.

Lesson Summary

To	Do this	Button
Set up Internet News, and select a news server	On the taskbar, click Start, point to Programs, and click Internet News. Follow the directions in the dialog box, and click Next when you finish adding information.	
View newsgroups	On the Internet News toolbar, click the Newsgroups button.	
Search for newsgroups	On the Internet News toolbar, click the Newsgroups icon. In the Display Newsgroups Which Contain box, type all or part of the name of the newsgroup you want to find.	Newsgroups

To	Do this	Button
Subscribe to a newsgroup	Select a newsgroup, and then click the Subscribe button.	
Clear the display to show all newsgroups	On the toolbar, click the Newsgroups button. Select any text in the Display Newsgroups Which Contain box, and then press DELETE.	
Open a newsgroup	Select a newsgroup, and then click the Go To button.	
Read articles	Click the article, and view it in the Preview pane. *or* Double-click the article.	
Follow a thread	When the article is open, click the Previous button or the Next button.	
Expand a thread	Click the plus sign next to an article icon.	
Print an article	On the toolbar, click the Print button.	
Save an article in the Saved Items folder	Select an article. On the File menu, click Save Message. Click OK.	
Delete an article	Select the article, and then on the File menu, click Delete.	
Save an article to your computer	Open the article. On the File menu, click Save As, select the folder for the file, select the name of the file, and then click the Save button.	
Reply to a newsgroup	Select an article. On the toolbar, click the Reply To Group button. Type a message, and then click the Post Message button.	Reply to Group
Create a new message	Click the New Message button. In the Newsgroup box, type the newsgroup name. In the Subject box, type a subject. In the message box, type a message, and then click the Post Message button.	New Message

For online information about	On the Help menu, click Help Topics. In the Help Topics dialog box, click Index, and then type
Viewing newsgroups	**viewing messages**
Searching for newsgroups	**finding newsgroups**
Subscribing to a newsgroup	**subscribing to newsgroups**
Opening a newsgroup	**opening,** and then display Messages
Reading articles	**reading messages**
Expanding a thread	**threads,** and then display Collapsing *or* Expanding
Printing an article	**printing messages**
Deleting an article	**deleting,** and then display Messages
Replying to a newsgroup	**replying to messages**
Creating a new message	**creating,** and then display Newsgroup messages

Meeting on the Internet

Estimated time
35 min.

In this lesson you will learn how to:

- Host meetings on the Internet.
- Share files and programs with other Microsoft NetMeeting users.
- Use the Whiteboard to sketch and display illustrations that support your ideas.

You're going to hold a business meeting that will be attended by participants from around the world. You coordinate the meeting so that everyone can be present at the designated location, on the specific day, at the specific time. At this meeting, you give each participant printouts of your presentation and other pertinent documents. During the meeting, the agenda topics are discussed. This scenario isn't so hard to imagine; meetings like this happen every day.

Now imagine that you can hold a meeting on the same date, at the same time, attended by the same participants, and hand out the same printouts of the same documents, without leaving your office. Even better, none of the other participants has to leave his or her office either. Science fiction? Not at all. Welcome to the technology of today! Using Microsoft NetMeeting, you can do all that and more.

NetMeeting is a tool that helps you conduct meetings over the Internet. Using NetMeeting, you can share your files and programs with co-workers, host live meetings over the Internet, carry on audio or written conversations, and illustrate your ideas by using an online "whiteboard."

NOTE Most of NetMeeting's features are available if you are using a modem or a local area network (LAN), but audio conversations are possible only if you and the person you're calling are both on a network; however, you don't have to be on the same network. If you aren't sure whether you're on a network, check with your system administrator or your Internet service provider. To learn more about using audio conversations on NetMeeting, refer to the One Step Further section at the end of this lesson.

Setting the Scene

 IMPORTANT To set up NetMeeting, refer to Appendix B, "Setting Up Internet Mail, Internet News, and NetMeeting."

At Fitch & Mather, you and your advertising team have been working hard on the Amazing Mouse campaign. Now you're ready to present your campaign ideas to Awesome Computers. The members of the decision-making group at Awesome Computers are based around the country. You decide to use NetMeeting to give your presentation because you can reach the greatest number of attendees at one time.

Start Microsoft NetMeeting

 IMPORTANT To learn how to use NetMeeting, you need to work with one or more people who also have NetMeeting installed. Have a co-worker or friend start NetMeeting on his or her computer and follow the lesson with you.

1   On your taskbar, click Start, and then point to Programs.
2   Click Microsoft NetMeeting.

   The NetMeeting window opens. From this window, you can work anywhere in NetMeeting.

3   Maximize the NetMeeting window. Your screen should look similar to the following illustration.

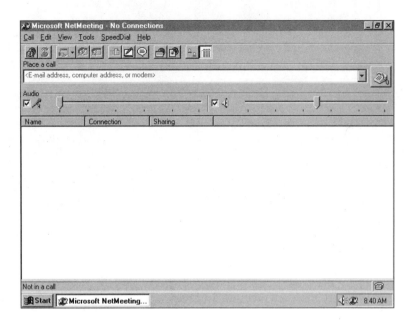

Calling Other NetMeeting Users

When you telephone someone, you perform a series of actions to achieve your goal. First, you pick up the receiver and listen for the dial tone, and then you dial the number. If the line is busy, you usually try to place your call again later. If the phone rings, you wait for the person on the other end to pick up the receiver and start speaking. When you and the person on the other end of the line have finished speaking, you both hang up.

Using NetMeeting is similar to making a phone call. In NetMeeting, instead of rotating a dial or pushing some buttons, you type an e-mail address, computer address, or modem number to place your call. Then, several things can happen, depending on what is going on at the other end of the line. If the other person does not have NetMeeting or doesn't have NetMeeting open, your call will not go through and the recipient has no way of knowing that you tried to call. If the other person has NetMeeting and the program is running, a dialog box opens on the recipient's screen stating that someone is trying to call. The person receiving the call can accept or ignore the call. If the person accepts your call, you are connected. If the person decides not to take your call, a message appears on your screen, stating that your call has not been accepted.

When someone is trying to call you, a message appears just above the status bar. To accept the call, click Accept; to reject the call, click Ignore.

In NetMeeting, you can place a call to one or to several NetMeeting users. To call another user, you can type the e-mail address, computer address, or modem telephone number in the Place A Call box. If you are calling multiple users, you can type all the addresses, separated by semi-colons, in the Place A Call box. Placing a NetMeeting call is similar to placing a telephone call, including the ability to speed-dial. To speed-dial in NetMeeting, instead of typing the addresses of multiple users, you can use the User Location Service (ULS) directory to select the person you want to call. When you click the person's name, his or her address appears in the Place A Call box. No typing is necessary!

How can you be listed on the ULS? When you install NetMeeting on your computer, you are asked if you want to be listed in the User Location Service directory. If you click yes, then when you start NetMeeting, you are automatically logged on to a Microsoft server. This server has the ULS directory running on it; the ULS is your NetMeeting telephone book. The ULS lists people who are running NetMeeting on their computers at that moment. The log-in name, real name, e-mail address, city, and country of each of the other NetMeeting users are displayed, similar to the listings in a telephone book. After you find the e-mail address you want, you can select the address and then click the Call button. Your call is dialed automatically.

 IMPORTANT When you install NetMeeting, the uls.microsoft.com server is configured as the default server. This server is often overcrowded; however, other servers are available. Use the same address and add a 1, 2, 3, 4, or 5 to the ULS as, for example, ULS1.microsoft.com. You can change your default server. On the Tools menu, click Options. Click the My Information tab. Select the User Location Service Name box contents, and then type the new server address. Click OK.

Call a NetMeeting user

While working on the Amazing Mouse campaign presentation, you need to communicate with one of your co-workers. During the call, you share documents, files, and illustrations. In this exercise, you will call your co-worker to discuss some art work.

 IMPORTANT For you to complete this lesson, your co-worker must accept your call. A dialog box appears on your co-worker's computer telling him or her that you are trying to call. Your co-worker should click the Accept button.

1 On the toolbar, click the Directory button.

The Directory dialog box appears.

Directory

2   Click the Directory down arrow, and then click uls.microsoft.com.

The User Location Service list is displayed.

3   Scroll down, and click your co-worker's e-mail address.

4   Click Call.

A message appears on your co-worker's screen stating that you are calling.

Accepting Messages Automatically

Using NetMeeting, you can set up your meeting so that incoming calls can be accepted automatically. When you have NetMeeting set up to accept calls automatically, you can't screen the calls; anyone can join the conversation. Because your e-mail address and your NetMeeting address are the same, if you don't list your address on the server when you install NetMeeting on your computer, your e-mail/NetMeeting address is unlisted, just like an unlisted telephone number. If you are unlisted, you'll probably want to give your address to co-workers and friends so you can communicate with them on NetMeeting. So that you don't miss any important calls, you might want to set up NetMeeting so that you can accept calls automatically. Keep in mind that "anyone," however, means that absolutely anyone who has an Internet connection and NetMeeting installed on his or her computer can join your conversation unless you select the Do Not Disturb option.

TIP   To prevent unwanted calls, you can select the Do Not Disturb option. When you select the Do Not Disturb option, the caller sees a message on his or her screen stating that you did not accept the call. To select the Do Not Disturb option, on the Call menu, click Do Not Disturb. A check mark appears next to the menu option. When you want to receive calls again, simply click Do Not Disturb again.

Accept calls automatically

You can determine if you want to accept all calls or to screen calls. In this exercise, you change your NetMeeting options so that calls are automatically accepted.

1   On the Tools menu in the NetMeeting window, click Options, and then verify that the General tab is in front.

2   Under Incoming Calls, select the Automatically Accept Calls When I'm Not In A Conference check box.

3   Click OK.

Your changes are saved, and you're returned to the NetMeeting window. To see how NetMeeting accepts calls for you automatically, have a third co-worker or friend call you using NetMeeting.

TIP Even if you do not have NetMeeting running, you can be notified when someone is trying to call you. On the Tools menu, click Options. Select the Run When Windows Starts And Notify Me Of Incoming Calls check box. Click OK.

Setting Up a Chat Area

Chat areas, sometimes referred to as chat rooms, are in *real-time*. That means you are reading messages as they arrive in the chat room and can respond to them immediately, with only a few seconds lag time between posting, reading, and responding. When you finish responding, another person can immediately answer. On the Internet, this immediacy is known as *real-time communications*.

Chat areas are most often set up on an online service, such as The Microsoft Network, but sometimes you can find a chat area as part of a Web site. The main function of a chat area is to be a gathering place for people who have similar interests. For instance, a Cat chat room is a place on the Internet where individuals who enjoy the company of their feline friends can go to exchange health care information, share cute anecdotes and, in general, brag about their pets. Often, a chat room can appear chaotic to the uninitiated. A chat area can contain you and one other person, or it can contain numerous individuals. When there are a large number of participants in a chat area, everyone appears to be speaking at the same time.

In NetMeeting, if you want to have a conversation with one or more individuals, then you have to create a chat area, which will allow you to carry on a written conversation in real-time. If more than two people are participating in a NetMeeting call, then all the participants can conduct a conversation in the chat area at the same time.

Set up a chat area

In this exercise, you set up a chat area in NetMeeting so that you and your co-worker can converse in real-time.

Chat

➤ On the toolbar, click the Chat button.

The Chat window opens. The insertion point is in the bottom pane. Your screen should look similar to the following illustration.

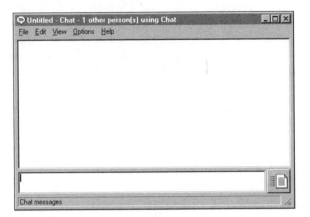

The Chat window is composed of two panes and an Enter button. The large pane displays the conversation between all the callers. The interaction takes place in this pane; everyone participating in the meeting can view its contents. The bottom pane, the message area pane, is where you type your messages. Only you can see the contents of this pane. When you have finished typing your message, you send your message to the chat area. Your message then appears in the conversation pane so that everyone participating in the meeting can read it.

Send a message

In this exercise, you use the Chat window to send a message to your co-worker.

1 Type **Hello. I'm glad you can attend this meeting. Beth Yamada finished the final art work and we're ready to present to Awesome Computers.**

2 Click the Enter button next to the bottom message area pane.

Your message appears in the main window of the chat area where the person you're connected to can read it. Your name appears to the left of the message, indicating who sent the message.

3 Have some fun here. You and your co-worker can practice sending messages to each other.

Enter

Saving a Chat

During formal business meetings, someone is usually assigned to keep the *minutes*, which are notes about what happens in the meeting. Minutes describe what happened at the meeting, what decisions were made, and what tasks were assigned to whom.

In NetMeeting, you can create the equivalent of meeting minutes by saving a complete transcript of every message that appeared in the chat area. What's even better, you don't have to supply copies to anyone: each attendee can save his or her own copy of all the chat messages.

Save chat messages

After completing your meeting, you decide to save the chat messages. In this exercise, you'll save the messages to your Desktop.

1   In the Chat window, on the File menu, click Save As.

The Save As dialog box appears.

2   Click the Save In down arrow, and then click Desktop.

3   In the File Name box, type your co-worker's name, and then click Save.

Your minutes are saved, and the dialog box closes.

NOTE   NetMeeting automatically adds a .csv file extension to any chats that you save.

4   Close the Chat window.

Sketching Ideas on the Whiteboard

Whiteboards are an integral part of many meetings these days. A *whiteboard* is a board made of a special material that you can write or draw on using water-washable markers. You can use a whiteboard as a tool to help get your point across.

To make your meeting more successful, NetMeeting contains a Whiteboard tool that you can use to display text, pictures, and drawings. In fact, you can do almost everything on the NetMeeting Whiteboard that you can do on a 3-dimensional whiteboard. You can mark up pictures, use a pointer to draw attention to different areas, and draw lines, squares, and circles. All the people participating in a NetMeeting meeting are able to view the Whiteboard—anyone can draw on it, even simultaneously.

Display the Whiteboard

You decide to display the Whiteboard so you can suggest some changes in the Awesome Computer logo.

Whiteboard

➤   On the NetMeeting toolbar, click the Whiteboard button.

The Whiteboard window opens. Your screen should look similar to the following illustration.

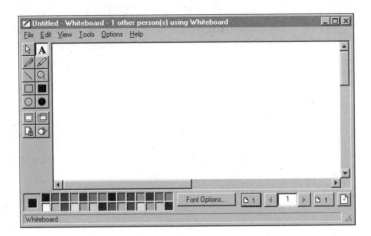

The Whiteboard window looks similar to many graphics program windows. A Drawing toolbar is positioned to the left of the main viewing area. Depending upon which tool you are using, a color palette appears at the bottom of the window.

Open an image in the Whiteboard

In this exercise, you open a NetMeeting file that displays the Awesome Computer advertising approval procedures so that you and your co-worker can add to the file.

1   In the Whiteboard window, on the File menu, click Open.

The Open dialog box appears.

2   Be sure the Microsoft Internet Explorer 3.0 Step by Step CD-ROM is in your CD-ROM drive. Click the Look In down arrow, and double-click the letter of your CD-ROM drive.

3   Click on Awesome, and then click Open.

The dialog box closes, and the graphic appears in the Whiteboard window. While viewing the graphic, you want to add a filled rectangle and add the words Fitch and Mather to the new image.

Filled Rectangle

4   On the Drawing toolbar, click the Filled Rectangle button.

The pointer turns into a crosshair pointer, and a color palette appears at the bottom of the window.

5   On the color palette, click the color you want to use.

6   Below the Research and Development box, drag the crosshair to create a rectangle.

A solid color rectangle appears in the Whiteboard window.

TIP You can also display an area of your computer screen or a program window in the Whiteboard window. On the Drawing toolbar, click the Select Window button. A message indicates that the next window you click will appear in the Whiteboard window. Click OK, and then click the window you want to display. If you want to display a portion of the screen or window, click the Select Area button, and then select the area you want.

Text

7 Click the Text button, and then click on the rectangle you just created.

8 In the box, type **Fitch and Mather**

Have some fun here. Use the tools in the Whiteboard window to change the image.

Saving the Contents of the Whiteboard

If you use NetMeeting, you can save drawings and images that were created during the meeting. Using the Whiteboard window, you can save the contents of the Whiteboard to your disk so that you can refer back to the material whenever you want.

Save the contents of the Whiteboard

In this exercise, you save your markups of the Whiteboard so that you can file them with your project files.

1 On the File menu, click Save As.

The Save As dialog box appears.

2 Click the Save In down arrow, and then select the Desktop.

3 In the File Name box, type **Markup** and then click Save.

The image, including your changes, is saved to your Desktop, and the dialog box closes. NetMeeting automatically adds the .wht filename extension to the filename.

TIP As you draw using the Whiteboard window, you can clear the Whiteboard during your meeting or you can wait to clear the Whiteboard until you quit NetMeeting. On the Edit menu, click Clear Page. A message box appears asking if you're sure you want to clear the whole page. Click Yes. The contents of the Whiteboard are deleted.

4 Close the Whiteboard window.

Sending Files

A common practice at meetings is to hand out copies of the presentation and the agenda before the meeting begins. In addition, meeting participants might have documents that they want to share with the other attendees. You could mail these documents in advance, but often they aren't ready until right before the meeting. Using NetMeeting, you can distribute your handouts quickly and inexpensively as files that arrive in a matter of minutes on the attendees' computers.

Send a file

In the next exercise, you send your co-worker a copy of the Awesome Computers' Stats file to refer to during the meeting.

Send File

1   On the NetMeeting toolbar, click the Send File button.

   The Select A File To Send dialog box appears.

2   Verify that the Microsoft Internet Explorer 3.0 Step by Step CD-ROM is listed in the Drive box. Double-click the CD-ROM drives and then select the Stats file.

3   Click Send.

   The dialog box appears, and the file is automatically sent to your co-worker. NetMeeting notifies you when the file is successfully delivered.

 TIP   The file is automatically sent to everyone in the call. If you want to send the file to only one meeting member, right-click that member's icon in the NetMeeting window. Click Send File. Select a file, and then click Send.

---

4   Click OK.

   A message appears on the recipient's Desktop asking whether the file should be opened, deleted, or saved.

 IMPORTANT   The Transfer Complete dialog box appears on your practice partner's computer indicating that a file is being downloaded. The recipient clicks the Open button to display the file.

 TROUBLESHOOTING   If you do not have the program that was used to create the received file, a message requests that you identify a program in which the file can be opened. For instance, the practice file in this exercise was created in Microsoft Word. If you don't have Word, then when the Open With dialog box opens, select Notepad.

Sharing Programs with Others

Imagine you're writing a book with the assistance of another person. Your collaborator lives on the other side of the country. When you complete a chapter, you send the chapter as an e-mail attachment or you mail a printout. When the chapter is delivered, the recipient marks up the document, adds text, removes text, and reorganizes the paragraphs. Your collaborator then sends the chapter back to you—using e-mail or *snail mail* (Internet jargon for the Postal Service). When you receive the document, you call your co-author to discuss the changes.

Using NetMeeting, you can bypass all this back-and-forth stuff and edit the document at the same time. If you and your co-author are in NetMeeting, you can open your document in, for example, Microsoft Word and the other person—even if he or she doesn't have Microsoft Word—can work on the document. You can actually see the editing changes while they are happening! You can share your programs with one other person or everyone in a meeting.

While you work on the document, the other attendees cannot work on it. This is known as *document control*. When you give up control of the document, another person can take control.

Share a program

In this exercise, you share Microsoft Internet Explorer with your co-worker.

1   Start Internet Explorer.

    The Internet Explorer window opens; your Custom Start Page is displayed.

2   In the Internet Explorer window, click the Minimize button.

    The NetMeeting window reappears.

*Share
Application*

3   On the NetMeeting toolbar, click the Share Application button.

    Any open programs (except NetMeeting) are listed.

4   Click Microsoft Internet Explorer.

    A message warns you that you are sharing an application and that you should be aware of the security risks.

5   Click OK.

    The Internet Explorer window and the Start Page open on your co-worker's screen.

Collaborate

6   On the toolbar in NetMeeting, click the Collaborate button.

    A message warns you that the individuals with whom you are sharing the program can use all the features of the program and that you should be careful when sharing programs with others.

IMPORTANT   The person you are collaborating with must also click the Collaborate button in his or her NetMeeting window.

7   Click OK.

The message closes, and the NetMeeting window opens.

 TIP   If you do not want to collaborate any longer, click the Work Alone button on the NetMeeting toolbar. A dialog box opens asking if you want to work alone. Click Yes.

Collaborating on Documents

After you and the other person have both clicked the Collaborate buttons in your respective NetMeeting windows, you can begin working on the file together. If you type, delete, copy, or paste in the file, the other person's mouse pointer freezes. When the other person attempts to move the pointer, a note next to the insertion point indicates "Click The Mouse To Take Control." You can click anywhere onscreen to take control of the mouse pointer. If the other person clicks anywhere onscreen, he or she "takes control" of the pointer, and is the only person who can work on the file; your pointer is frozen until you take control by clicking anywhere onscreen again. When collaborating on a document, it's a good idea to take turns working on it. Otherwise, you and your partner might end up spending more time warring over the pointer than working on the document. In addition, when both of you are working on the document together, you cannot see what the other person is doing and you can end up working at cross-purposes.

 WARNING   Your collaborator is able to use all the features of the program. Keep in mind that the other person can, through your program window, open any unprotected files created in the shared program.

Review a document

In this exercise, you let your co-worker browse the World Wide Web using your Internet Explorer window.

Turn to Lesson 1, "Traveling the World Wide Web," for more information about how to browse Web pages.

1 Switch to the Custom Start Page in the Internet Explorer window.

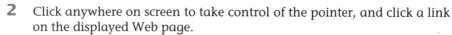

IMPORTANT To collaborate, let your co-worker take control of the pointer. Your co-worker needs to click anywhere onscreen. Your pointer freezes. Your co-worker scrolls down and selects a Web page link.

2 Click anywhere on screen to take control of the pointer, and click a link on the displayed Web page.

3 On the NetMeeting toolbar, click the Work Alone button.

Your collaborator cannot make any selections on the Web page now.

Work Alone

4 Experiment with collaborating and working alone. When you're ready, go to step 5.

5 On the Internet Explorer toolbar, click the Home button, and on the Internet Explorer window, click the Close button.

Home

Ending a Call

When you and your co-worker have finished working on NetMeeting, you need to end the call. Ending a call in NetMeeting by clicking a button is the equivalent of hanging up a telephone receiver.

End a call

In this exercise, you will end your call to your co-worker.

➤ On the NetMeeting toolbar, click the Hang Up button.

You and your co-worker are disconnected from the call.

Hang Up

Hosting a Meeting

In the business world, meetings are a fact of life. Meetings are held to update a group of team members on projects, to make company-wide decisions, to determine policies, and for a myriad of other reasons. There are usually more than two participants in a meeting. The team leader or member usually calls the meeting. The person who calls the meeting together usually determines the date, time, and location of the meeting; selects the attendees; and sets or organizes the agenda. Also, this person usually leads when the meeting begins.

Just as a face-to-face meeting has a host, so does a NetMeeting meeting. The primary job of the NetMeeting host is to set up the chat area for the meeting. To become a meeting host, you select the Host Conference option and open the chat area. Then, the other meeting attendees must call you if they want to join the meeting.

IMPORTANT To learn how to host a meeting, you should work with more than two people. Before continuing with this exercise, organize a meeting with a group of co-workers or friends who all have NetMeeting installed on their computers. Then you host the meeting and have all the meeting attendees call you.

Host a meeting

You and your co-workers are going to meet using NetMeeting. In this exercise, you'll be the host. You set up a chat area where you can conduct your NetMeeting.

1   On the Call menu, click Host Conference.

    A message appears telling you that the conference will end when you hang up and that either anyone who calls can join the conference or you can screen calls. You can accept a call during a meeting by clicking the Accept button in the Incoming Call box.

2   Click OK.

    A list of meeting participants is displayed in the main area of the NetMeeting window as meeting members join the meeting. The names of your co-workers should appear in the NetMeeting window as they call to join the meeting and you accept their calls. You can all collaborate on files, use the Whiteboard, communicate in the chat area, and share programs using NetMeeting just as you learned in earlier exercises.

Disconnecting from a Meeting

As the meeting host, you have two ways to disconnect meeting participants. You can disconnect yourself and all the meeting participants, or you can disconnect an individual.

TIP If you're not the meeting host, you can disconnect at any point by clicking the HangUp button on the NetMeeting toolbar.

End a meeting

In this exercise, you end a meeting and disconnect all the attendees.

TIP You can disconnect a single participant from a meeting. Right-click the name of the person you want to disconnect in the NetMeeting window and then click Disconnect.

1 In the NetMeeting window, click the Chat button.

The chat window opens.

Enter

2 In the message pane, type **Thank you for participating in this meeting. We'll meet again in two weeks to discuss our progress. I'm going to disconnect the meeting now. Then click the Enter button.**

3 In the chat window, click the Close button.

A message box appears asking if you want to save the current list of messages.

4 Click No.

The chat window closes and the NetMeeting window is active again.

Hang Up

5 On the toolbar, click the Hang Up button.

The meeting is ended, and all the meeting participants are disconnected from the chat room.

NOTE   If you'd like to build on the skills that you learned in this lesson, you can do the One Step Further. Otherwise, skip to "Finish the lesson."

One Step Further: Using Your Voice on the Internet

If you have a sound card, computer speakers, a microphone, and a TCP/IP connection, you can use NetMeeting's audio features. You can actually use your computer to have an audio conversation with other meeting members. However, unlike the unlimited participation allowed in chat areas or program sharing, only two computers can be connected for audio to work properly, regardless of the number of people in a NetMeeting meeting.

IMPORTANT   If you are unsure whether you have a TCP/IP line, check with your system administrator. If you use a modem, you cannot use the NetMeeting audio features. For more information about TCP/IP connections, see Lesson 1, "Traveling the World Wide Web."

Placing a Call by Using Audio

Using NetMeeting, you can call anyone and speak with that person through your computers as long as you both have TCP/IP connections and both your computers have sound cards, speakers, and microphones. Placing a call by using audio in NetMeeting requires more information than simply calling another person. Calls that use audio are called advanced calls. An *advanced call* is

NetMeeting's term for a call that requires additional information. To place an advanced call, you need to open the Advanced Calling dialog box and make some selections.

Place an advanced call

You and your co-worker have TCP/IP lines and you want to talk with each other while you use the Whiteboard and share programs. In this exercise, you place an advanced call to your co-worker's computer.

 IMPORTANT Keep your TCP/IP line number on hand because you'll need to use it for this exercise. If you don't know the number, ask your system administrator.

1   On the Call menu, click Place Advanced Call.

    The Advanced Calling dialog box appears.

2   Under Calling, click the Call Using down arrow, and click Network (TCP/IP).

3   In the Address box, type your TCP/IP line number.

If you want to only speak with the person, then click the Audio Only option.

4   Select the Both Audio And Data option.

    This option allows you to send and receive messages, share programs and files, and send files.

5   Click Call.

    Your co-worker should hear a telephone ringing on his or her computer. To accept the call, your co-worker clicks the Accept button.

 TIP To disconnect an advanced call, click the Hang Up button on the NetMeeting toolbar.

Finish the lesson

1   On the Desktop, hold down the SHIFT key, click the Sample Chat file, and then click the Sample Markup file. Use the right mouse button to click one of the highlighted files, and then click Delete.

    The Confirm File Delete dialog box appears asking whether you're sure you want to delete the files.

2   Click Yes.

    The files are deleted.

3   If you are finished using NetMeeting, in the NetMeeting window, click the Close button.

141

Lesson Summary

To	Do this	Button
Call a NetMeeting user	Click the Directory button. Click the Directory down arrow, and then click uls.microsoft.com. Select an address. Click the Call button.	
Accept a NetMeeting call	Click Accept.	
Host a meeting	On the Call menu, click Host Conference. Click OK.	
Set up a chat area	On the toolbar, click the Chat button.	
Disconnect an individual from a meeting	In the NetMeeting window, use the right mouse button to click the name of the person you want to disconnect, and then click Disconnect.	
Send a message	In the Chat window, type in the message area pane. Click the Enter button.	
Accept calls automatically when in a conference	In the NetMeeting window, on the Tools menu, click Options. Click the General tab. Under Incoming Calls, select the Automatically Accept Calls When I'm Participating In A Conference check box. Click OK.	
End a meeting	On the NetMeeting toolbar, click the Hang Up button.	
Save chat messages	In the Chat window, click Save As on the File menu. Click the Save In down arrow, and then select the appropriate place to save the file. In the File Name box, type a filename, and then click Save.	
Display the Whiteboard	On the NetMeeting toolbar, click the Whiteboard button.	
Open an image in the Whiteboard	In the Whiteboard window, on the File menu, click Open. Click the Look In down arrow, and then select the file you want to open.	

To	Do this	Button
Save the contents of the Whiteboard	On the File menu, click Save As. Click the Save In down arrow, and then select Desktop. In the File Name box, type a name, and then click Save.	
Clear the Whiteboard	On the Edit menu, click Clear Page. Close the Whiteboard window.	
Send a file	On the NetMeeting toolbar, click the Send File button. Select a file, and then click Send. Click OK.	
Open a received file	On the Transfer Complete dialog box, click Open.	
Share a program	Open the program you want to share. On the NetMeeting toolbar, click the Share Application button. Click the program name, and then click OK.	
Collaborate using a program	In the NetMeeting window, click the Collaborate button, and then click OK.	

For online information about	**On the Help menu, click Help Topics. In the Help Topics dialog box, click Index, and then type**
Calling other NetMeeting users	**calls** or **calling**
Hosting a meeting	**hosting a conference**
Disconnecting from a meeting	**disconnecting yourself from a meeting,** or **ending a call**
Setting up a chat area	**chat,** and then display Starting
Using the whiteboard	**whiteboard**
Sending and opening files	**sending,** and then display Files
Sharing programs	**sharing applications** or **program sharing**

Review & Practice

Estimated time
20 min.

You will review and practice how to:

- Create and send e-mail
- Create and post a newsgroup article
- Arrange a meeting by using NetMeeting

Before you complete this book, you can practice the skills you learned in Part 2 by working through this Review & Practice section. You will use Internet Mail to create a message to a co-worker, and then send the message, you will create a newsgroup article, and finally, you will arrange a meeting by using NetMeeting.

Scenario

Fitch & Mather's two biggest competitors have merged, and upper management is concerned about what this could mean for the future of the company. You have been asked to arrange a meeting with the other advertising executives to discuss their ideas on the subject. You decide to post articles to a newsgroup to get other advertising professionals' opinions on the subject. A day before the meeting, Fitch & Mather's main advertising executive is sent to Boston to meet with an important client, so you use NetMeeting to include that executive in the discussion.

Step 1: *Create an E-mail Message*

You have a list of several people you want to invite to the meeting. You send a e-mail message to your assistant with the list of advertising executives who should be there.

1 Start Internet Mail.

2 Address the e-mail to **Beth Yamada**.

3 Give the message the subject, **Ad Exec. Meeting**.

4 Type the message, **Please invite John Miller, Trinh Nguyen, and Stan Grikowski to a meeting this Friday at 2:30.**

5 Send the message.

6 Exit Internet Mail.

For more information about	See
Starting Internet Mail	Lesson 4
Addressing e-mail	Lesson 4
Entering message text	Lesson 4
Sending a message	Lesson 4

Step 2: *Create and Post a Newsgroup Article*

Now that the e-mail message has been sent to Beth to invite people to the meeting, you want to create and post a newsgroup message to get opinions from other advertising professionals.

1 Start Internet News, and then connect to the Internet if necessary.

2 Open the biz.general newsgroup.

3 Create a new message.

4 Give the message the subject, **F&B Merger**

5 Type the message, **What do people think of the Ferguson and Bardell merger?**

6 Post the message.

7 Exit Internet News.

For more information about	See
Starting Internet News	Lesson 5
Opening a newsgroup	Lesson 5
Creating a new message	Lesson 5
Posting a message	Lesson 5
Exiting Internet News	Lesson 5

Step 3: *Arrange a Meeting*

The meeting has been set up, and everyone is present, except for the advertising executive in Boston (have a co-worker who has NetMeeting on his or her computer assume this role). You start NetMeeting and include that executive in the meeting.

1   Start NetMeeting.
2   Make yourself the host of the meeting.
3   Connect with your partner through NetMeeting.
4   Start Chat.
5   Tell your partner that you are glad he or she could join the meeting.
6   Disconnect your partner from the meeting.
7   Exit NetMeeting, and then disconnect from the Internet if necessary.

For more information about	See
Starting NetMeeting	Lesson 6
Hosting a meeting	Lesson 6
Connecting with NetMeeting	Lesson 6
Using Chat	Lesson 6
Disconnecting from a meeting	Lesson 6
Exiting NetMeeting	Lesson 6

Finish the Review & Practice

1   Verify that you are disconnected from the Internet.
2   Open your Inbox, select the Ad. Exec. Meeting message, and then press DELETE.
3   Close all windows on the Desktop.

Appendixes

Setting Up Your Internet Connection

This appendix will take you step by step through the setup of The Microsoft Network and Microsoft Internet Explorer. You would be amazed at the myriad technical details you usually have to know to install an Internet connection: ISPs, DSNs, TCP/IP, bps, ports, and so on. Fortunately, Internet Explorer includes installation wizards, which are programs that automate the installation process, to help you connect with the Internet.

 IMPORTANT   If you are using Windows NT, you must use an Internet service provider other than The Microsoft Network. Unless you have Internet access through a network, contact an Internet service provider in your area and make arrangements for a dial-up Internet connection. Then skip to the section "Setting up an Internet service provider other than The Microsoft Network."

Setting Up Your Internet Connection

If you are using a network connection, skip to the "Installing Internet Explorer" section.

 IMPORTANT   Before you start using Internet Explorer, your modem or network connection should be set up. Use the Add New Hardware wizard in Control Panel to help you install and configure your modem. If you need help with your network connection, ask your system administrator to assist you.

- If you are signing up with The Microsoft Network or another Internet service provider to use Internet Explorer, you should install The Microsoft Network or your Internet service provider before you install Internet Explorer. Doing the setup in this order will make installation easier.

- If you are using an Internet service provider other than The Microsoft Network, you will have to create a Windows dial-up networking connection. Your Internet service provider should have the information you need to set up your computer to work with that service.

Setting Up Your MSN Account

Before you can sign on to The Microsoft Network, you must install the program on your computer. The Microsoft Network icon appears on your Windows Desktop if the program is installed. Otherwise, the Set Up The Microsoft Network icon appears on your Desktop. To install The Microsoft Network, double-click the Set Up The Microsoft Network icon and follow the instructions. If you have installed MSN and you do not see The Microsoft Network icon, restart your computer.

Set up The Microsoft Network

The Microsoft
Network

*You can also
click the Start
button on the
taskbar, point
to Programs,
and then click
The Microsoft
Network.*

1 On the Desktop, double-click The Microsoft Network icon.

The Microsoft Network Wizard dialog box appears.

2 Click OK.

If you already have an account with The Microsoft Network, select the Click Here If You Are Already A Member Of The Microsoft Network check box before clicking OK. The next dialog box appears.

3 Be sure the Your Area Or City Code box contains the correct area code, type the first three digits of your phone number in The First Three Digits Of Your Phone Number box, and then click OK.

The next dialog box appears.

4 Click Connect.

The Pre-Dial Terminal Screen dialog box appears.

5 Click Continue.

The Microsoft Network Wizard determines the closest MSN provider in your area, and then transfers that information to your computer. The next dialog box appears.

6 Click Tell Us Your Name And Address, fill in all the boxes on the Tell Us Your Name And Address dialog box, and then click OK.

This information is used by MSN to set up your account.

7   Click the Next, Select A Way To Pay option, select the credit card of your choice, enter the required information, and then click OK.

8   Click the Then Please Read The Rules button, read the MSN, The Microsoft Network Member Agreement, and then click the I Agree button.

If you click I Disagree, you will not be able to sign up for MSN.

9   Click the Join Now button.

The next dialog box appears.

10   Click Connect.

The Pre-Dial Terminal Screen dialog box appears.

11   On the Pre-Dial Terminal Screen dialog box, click Continue.

The information you entered is sent by your modem to The Microsoft Network. The Microsoft Member ID And Password window opens.

Create your MSN account

Member names cannot include spaces.

1   In the Member ID box, type the identification name you would like to use, click in the Password box, type a password, and then click OK.

If someone already has the Member ID that you choose, you will be asked to enter another ID.

2   Be sure that that the Yes, I Want MSN w/Full Internet Access option is selected, and then click OK.

You must have full Internet access to use the World Wide Web.

You can avoid long-distance telephone charges by using a local access number.

3   Be sure that that the phone numbers selected are the closest to your location.

To change the phone number, click the Change button, and then select a different phone number.

4   Click OK, and then click Finish.

The Sign In dialog box appears.

5   If you want to connect to The Microsoft Network, type your Member ID in the Member ID box, type your password in the Password box, and then click Connect.

The Microsoft Network automatically sets up Microsoft Exchange, so you don't need to set up Exchange separately.

Setting Up an Internet Service Provider Other Than The Microsoft Network

Your Internet service provider might already have an information sheet detailing everything you need to set up a dial-up network connection using Windows 95 or Windows NT.

If you are using an Internet service provider other than The Microsoft Network, your Installation process is a little more complicated.

 NOTE Don't worry if you don't understand the terms in this section. Your Internet service provider representative knows what the terms mean.

Before you begin this procedure, you should have installed and tested the modem you will use to gain access to your Internet service provider. You should also have the following information from your Internet service provider:

- The name of the service.
- The telephone number to gain access to the Internet.
- The user name and password you will use with the service.
- Whether the service automatically assigns an Internet Protocol (IP) address when you log in. If not, you need the IP address and the Subnet Mask.
- The Internet Protocol address of your Domain Name Service (DNS) server, and an alternate address, if available.
- Your e-mail address and the address of your Internet mail server.

To set up your dial-up networking connection, double-click the My Computer icon on the Desktop, double-click the Dial-Up Networking icon, and then double-click the Make New Connection icon. Follow the steps of the Make New Connection wizard to set up your Internet service provider access.

 NOTE Some features of Internet Explorer 3.0 may not be available in your area if you are outside the U.S.

Installing Internet Explorer

Before you set up Internet Explorer 3.0, you must install the program by running the Internet Starter Kit on the Microsoft Internet Explorer 3.0 Step by Step CD-ROM or by downloading the most current copy of Internet Explorer 3.0 from http://www.microsoft.com/ie/download. Download the full installation of Internet Explorer, which includes Internet Mail and Internet News.

WARNING If you are using Microsoft Exchange as your messaging program, do not install the Internet Mail component of Internet Explorer. The two programs are used for different types of mail services. If you install Internet Mail, it will replace Exchange as your default e-mail program for all mail actions.

Install Internet Explorer for Windows 95

1 On the Desktop, double-click the My Computer icon.

2 Double-click the drive icon for your CD-ROM drive.

3 Double-click the Internet Explorer 3.0 folder, and then double-click the Setup icon.

The Microsoft Internet Explorer Starter Kit window opens.

If you do not see the Connect To The Web Now! link, click the Install Internet Explorer Starter Kit link, and proceed with steps 5 through 12 in the "Install Internet Explorer for Windows NT" section below.

4 Click the Connect To The Web Now! link.

5 Click the Internet Connection Wizard link.

6 Click the icon to start the Internet Connection Wizard.

7 Click Next.

The Setup Options dialog box of the Internet Connection wizard appears.

8 Skip to the "Set up Internet Explorer for Windows 95 and Windows NT" section.

Install Internet Explorer for Windows NT

1 On the Desktop, double-click on My Computer, and then double-click the drive icon for your CD-ROM drive.

2 Double-click the Internet Explorer 3.0 folder, double-click the Win95 folder, and then double-click the Eng folder.

3 Double-click the ie3inst icon.

The Internet Explorer Starter Kit dialog box opens.

4 Click the Install Internet Explorer Starter Kit link.

5 Read the End-User License Agreement for Microsoft Internet Explorer. If you accept the agreement, click Yes.

A message asks if you would like to choose which optional Internet components are installed.

6 Click Yes.

7 Clear the Internet Mail and Internet News check boxes.

There are special versions of these programs for Windows NT users.

8 Click OK.

9 When the Internet Explorer Starter Kit asks whether you want to restart your computer now, click Yes.

After your computer has restarted, the Internet Explorer Starter Kit is on the screen.

10 In the left column, click the Explore The Web link.

11 Scroll down, and in the right column, click the Click Here to Begin Your Journey link.

A message informs you that you are leaving the Internet Explorer Starter Kit to browse the Web live and asks whether you want to continue.

12 Click Yes.

Internet Explorer starts, and the Setup Options dialog box of the Internet Connection Wizard appears.

Set up Internet Explorer for Windows 95 and Windows NT

1 Click the Current option, and then click Next.

The Internet Connection wizard uses your current settings to set up Internet Explorer. If you have a network connection, it will set up Internet Explorer to work with your network. If you have MSN or a dial-up connection, the Internet Connection wizard will set up Internet Explorer to work with those connections.

2 Click the Exit link.

The Internet Explorer setup is complete, and Internet Explorer is ready for you to use.

Setting Up Internet Mail, Internet News, and NetMeeting

Before you can begin to work through the lessons presented in Part 2 of this book, you need to set up Microsoft Internet Mail, Microsoft Internet News, and Microsoft NetMeeting. These programs are available on the CD-ROM included with *Microsoft Internet Explorer 3.0 Step by Step*. You can also download Internet Explorer from the Microsoft Web site at http://www.microsoft.com/ie/download. Before you can use these programs to communicate over the Internet, you must configure them.

 IMPORTANT If you are using Windows NT, there are special versions of Internet Mail and Internet News written especially for your operating system. If you already have Internet Explorer up and running properly, go to the section, "Download Internet Mail and Internet News for Windows NT," and begin there.

Setting Up Internet Mail

Before you begin sending and receiving e-mail, you must set up Internet Mail. The messages you send and receive are typically stored on a server dedicated to e-mail. When a server receives a message, it is placed in an outgoing or incoming storage area until the message can be delivered to the recipient. Internet Mail handles outgoing and incoming mail using SMTP and POP3; therefore, you need to tell Internet Mail the name of your Internet service provider's e-mail server.

Set up Internet Mail

The Internet

1 On the Desktop, double-click The Internet icon.

Internet Explorer opens.

> ![] **IMPORTANT** You don't need to be online to set up Internet Mail or Internet News. To prevent Internet Explorer from connecting to your Internet service provider on startup, click the Stop button on the Internet Explorer toolbar if you access the Internet through a network, or click Cancel when Internet Explorer asks if you want to connect to your Internet service provider.

Mail

2 On the Internet Explorer toolbar, click the Mail button, and then click Read Mail.

The Internet Mail window opens, and the Internet Mail Configuration wizard appears.

3 Click Next.

The second page of the Internet Mail Configuration wizard appears.

4 In the Name box, type your name or the alias you want to use when sending e-mail. In the Email Address box, type your complete e-mail address, and then click Next.

The third page of the Internet Mail Configuration wizard appears.

Set up your mail server

If you're unsure of your service provider's e-mail server, contact your service provider.

1 In the Incoming Mail (POP3) Server box, type the name of the server that you are using for your incoming mail. In the Outgoing Mail (SMTP) Server box, type the name of the server that you are using for your outgoing mail, and then click Next.

The fourth page of the Internet Mail Configuration wizard appears.

If your e-mail address is bethy@www. fnm.com, for example, type bethy as your account name.

2 In the Email Account box, type your account name.

3 In the Password box, type the password you use to sign into your e-mail account. Click Next.

4 Select the type of connection you have:

- If you have a network connection, click the I Use A LAN Connection option, and skip to step 6.

- If you have a modem and you don't use dial-up networking, click the I Connect Manually option, and skip to step 6.

- If you want to be automatically connected to your news server when you start Internet News, click the I Use A Modem To Access My Email option, and go to step 5.

5   Click the Use The Following Dial Up Networking Connection down arrow, and then select your service provider.

6   Click Next, and then click Finish.

    The Internet Mail window opens. It contains an e-mail message welcoming you to Microsoft Internet Mail and Internet News. Now you're ready to communicate with anyone connected to the Internet.

7   If you are finished working with Internet Mail, then in the Internet Mail window, click the Close button. Otherwise, see Lesson 4 to learn how to use Internet Mail.

Setting Up Internet News

To view newsgroups, you need a *newsreader* installed on your computer. The newsreader allows you to gain access to a news server that has Usenet groups stored on it, and then displays the available newsgroups for you. Newsgroups are located on news servers throughout the world. You must know the location of a news server before you can connect to it. Typically, your Internet service provider has a news server that stores newsgroups. You must get that news server address from your service provider before you can continue with this section.

Set up Internet News

 IMPORTANT You need to know the name of your Internet service provider's newsgroup server before you begin setting up Internet News. If you do not know the server's name, contact your Internet service provider before continuing. If you are on a LAN, ask your system administrator for the name of your company's news server.

1   On the Internet Explorer toolbar, click the Mail button, and then click Read News.

    The Internet News Configuration wizard appears.

2   Click Next.

    The second page of the Internet News Configuration wizard appears.

3   In the Name box, type your name, press TAB, and then type your e-mail address in the Email Address box. Click Next.

    The third page of the Internet News Configuration wizard appears.

Set up your newsgroup server

1 In the News Server box, type the news server address that your service provider gave you, and then click Next.

The fourth page of the Internet News Configuration wizard appears.

 NOTE If your news server requires that you supply a password before you can read the newsgroups located on it, click the My News Server Requires Me To Logon check box. Either type your account name or number and password for the news server, or click Logon Using Secure Password Authentication.

2 Select the type of connection you have.

- If you have a network connection, click the I Use A LAN Connection option, and skip to step 4.

- If you have a modem *and* you want to start your modem manually because you don't have dial-up networking, click the I Connect Manually option, and skip to step 4.

- If you want to be automatically connected to your news server when you start Internet News. Click the I Use A Modem To Access My Newsgroups option, and go to step 3.

3 Click the Use The Following Dial-Up Networking Connection down arrow, and select your service provider.

4 Click Next, and then click Finish.

The Newsgroups dialog box appears. A message appears stating that newsgroups are being downloaded from the server you selected. Downloading newsgroups can take several moments, depending upon the number of newsgroups stored on the server.

5 If you are finished working with Internet News, close the Newsgroups dialog box, and then close the Internet News window. Otherwise, refer to Lesson 5 to learn how to use Internet News.

6 Close the Internet Explorer window.

Setting Up NetMeeting

Using NetMeeting, you can conduct meetings and conferences over the Internet or on a LAN. When you set up NetMeeting, the information you typed appears in the User Location Server (ULS), which is a directory of NetMeeting users, so anyone using NetMeeting can find you. By default, the ULS is uls.microsoft.com, which is located at Microsoft's offices in Redmond, Washing-

If you are changing your default server to your local network, ask your system administrator for assistance.

ton. You can use this server as your default or you can change the server to one of the other servers that are available through Microsoft—for example, uls5.microsoft.com. You can also change your default server to your local network.

 IMPORTANT   At the time this book went to press, NetMeeting was not available for Windows NT. Check the Microsoft Web site for updates of NetMeeting at http://www.microsoft.com/ie/download

Before you begin communicating in conferences using NetMeeting, you need to set up the NetMeeting program.

Install NetMeeting

1   On the Desktop, double-click the My Computer icon.

2   Double-click the drive icon for your CD-ROM drive.

3   Double-click the Internet Explorer 3.0 folder, and then double-click the Setup icon.

4   Click the Internet Extras link.

5   Click the NetMeeting link.

6   Scroll down, and then click the icon to install NetMeeting.

Set up NetMeeting

1   Click Start, point to Programs, and then click Microsoft NetMeeting.

The Microsoft NetMeeting wizard appears.

2   Click Next.

The Microsoft Internet User Location Service dialog box appears.

3   In the First Name box, type your first name, and then in the Last Name box, type your last name.

4   In the E-mail Address box, type your complete e-mail address.

- Optionally, in the City/State box, type the name of your city and state.

- Optionally, in the Country box, type the name of your country.

- Optionally, in the Comments box, type any comments that you want other NetMeeting users to read about you. For example, if you don't have voice capabilities, type No Voice.

5   Click Next.

Set up your User Location Server

1   To publish your name on a User Location Server, click the Yes option.

If you select No, you will not be listed in Microsoft's directory, and your address and name cannot be found by other users. If you are planning to use NetMeeting only within your company, for example, the No option might be preferable.

2   If you want to use a server other than the default, in the What Is The Name Of The User Location Server You Would Like To Use To Find People? box, type the name of the server you want to use.

 IMPORTANT   You can select the default server as your server now and then change it later. To change your default server, on the Tools menu, click Options. Click the My Information tab. In the User Location Service Name box, type the name of the server you want to use. Click OK.

3   Click Next.

The Audio Tuning Wizard configuration page appears. If your computer does not have a sound card, click Finish.

Tune your audio features

1   Click Next.

The second page of the Audio Tuning Wizard appears. Your sound card, if you have one, is automatically detected, and its name is displayed in the Recording and Playback boxes.

2   Click Next.

3   Under Specify The Speed Of Your Connection To The Network You Will Be Using To Make Microsoft NetMeeting Calls, select the type of connection that you have, and then click Next.

4   Click Start Recording, and then speak into your computer's microphone.

 IMPORTANT   If your computer doesn't have a speaker and microphone, click the Start Recording button anyway, and continue with step 5.

When the Tuning Progress box is completely blue, the wizard has finished tuning your audio features.

5   Click Next, and then click Finish.

Next.
NetMeeting opens on your Desktop.

6   If you are finished working with NetMeeting, close the NetMeeting window. Otherwise, refer to Lesson 6 to learn how to use NetMeeting.

Download Internet Mail and Internet News for Windows NT

1   Start Internet Explorer, if it is not already running.

2   Click in the Address box, then type **www.microsoft.com** and press ENTER.

The Microsoft Web site is displayed.

3   On the left side of the page, click the Free Downloads link.

4   Scroll down the page until you find the heading "Internet Technologies."

5   Click the Internet Mail And News 1.0 For Windows NT link, then follow the instructions for downloading the programs.

Microsoft asks which additional features and components you would like to download.

6   Click the right arrow in the drop-down list box, and then choose Microsoft Internet Mail And News For Windows NT 4.0. Click Next.

7   Be sure that the language selection is correct, and then click Next.

Internet Explorer displays a list of download sites.

8   Choose the site closest to you, and click the Mailnews.exe link next to that site.

The file starts downloading to your computer, and a message asks where you want to save the file.

9   Be sure the Save It To Disk option is selected, and then click OK.

10   When Internet Explorer asks where you want to save the file, be sure that the Save In box indicates Desktop, and then click Save.

The file finishes downloading to your computer.

11   Minimize the Internet Explorer window.

12   On the Desktop, double-click the Mailnews icon.

13   Read the End User Agreement and, if you agree, click Yes.

The Internet Mail And News wizard begins. Go back to step 4 of the "Set up Internet Mail" section to finish installing Internet Mail and Internet News on your computer.

Index

A

acronyms, standard, 119
ActiveX, 39
Address box, Internet Explorer, 14, 15
addresses
    adding to Address Book, 82–83
    using Address Book, 84–85
    World Wide Web syntax, 8–9
addressing e-mail messages, 83–85
Address toolbar, 41
advanced calls, 140–41
AltaVista, 55, 59
Alternative (alt) Usenet category, 105
anti-virus software, 22
applications, sharing in NetMeeting, 136–37
articles, newsgroup. *See* messages, newsgroup
attached files
    adding to e-mail messages, 96–97
    identifying by icon, 93
audio feature, NetMeeting
    configuring, 162
    using in meetings, 140–41
Audio Tuning Wizard, 164
Authenticode, 39

B

Back button, 14
Bill Nye Web site, 36
bitmaps, defined, 24
BMP files, 24, 25
browsers, 6. *See also* Internet Explorer
browsing
    e-mail messages, 93–94
    Web pages, 10–13
Business (biz) Usenet category, 107
business meetings, online. *See* NetMeeting

C

calling NetMeeting users, 127–29. *See also* audio feature, NetMeeting
carbon copy messages, 84
case, importance in URLs, 12
CC messages, 84
certificates, 49
chat rooms. *See also* audio feature, NetMeeting
    defined, 102
    in NetMeeting, 130–32
    saving NetMeeting chat, 131–32
colors
    changing in Internet Explorer window, 45
    difference after viewing links, 16
    overriding default colors for Web links, 45
compressed files
    decompressing, 21
    defined, 21, 98
    downloading, 21
    vs. encoded files, 98
    using, 97, 98
Computer Network Web site, 37
Computers (comp) Usenet category, 107
computer viruses, 22, 49
com sites, 11
concepts, searching by on WWW, 60–63
Content Advisor, 68–70
conversations. *See* audio feature, NetMeeting; chat rooms; real-time communication
cookies, 49
crawlers, 54, 56
Custom Start Page
    adding links, 36
    creating, 34–38
    overview, 32
    saving as default Start Page, 38
    selecting basic services, 35

Custom Start Page, *continued*
    selecting site categories, 36
    setting up, 34–38

D

Debate-oriented (talk) Usenet category, 107
decompressing files, 21, 23, 98
Deleted Items folder, 87, 95–96
deleting
    e-mail messages, 95–96
    newsgroup messages, 113
Desktop
    creating Internet links on, 28
    creating wallpaper from Web graphics, 46–47
    saving files to, 23
    saving newsgroup messages to, 116
dial-up connections. *See also* Internet service providers; Microsoft Network, The
    defined, 6
    vs. network connections, 6
    setting up, 153–56
documents, collaborating on, 137–40
downloading files, 20, 21, 22, 48–49

E

edu sites, 11
electronic mail. *See* e-mail
e-mail. *See also* messages, e-mail
    overview, 79–80
    using Internet Mail, 80–99
    using Microsoft Exchange, 86, 88, 89, 92, 96
e-mail addresses, and NetMeeting, 128
emoticons, 116–17
encoded files, 98
error messages, 9
etiquette, newsgroup, 114–17

IMPORTANT—READ CAREFULLY BEFORE OPENING SOFTWARE PACKET(S). By opening the sealed packet(s) containing the software, you indicate your acceptance of the following Microsoft License Agreement.

MICROSOFT LICENSE AGREEMENT

(Book Companion CD)

This is a legal agreement between you (either an individual or an entity) and Microsoft Corporation. By opening the sealed software packet(s) you are agreeing to be bound by the terms of this agreement. If you do not agree to the terms of this agreement, promptly return the unopened software packet(s) and any accompanying written materials to the place you obtained them for a full refund.

MICROSOFT SOFTWARE LICENSE

1. GRANT OF LICENSE. Microsoft grants to you the right to use one copy of the Microsoft software program included with this book (the "SOFTWARE") on a single terminal connected to a single computer. The SOFTWARE is in "use" on a computer when it is loaded into the temporary memory (i.e., RAM) or installed into the permanent memory (e.g., hard disk, CD-ROM, or other storage device) of that computer. You may not network the SOFTWARE or otherwise use it on more than one computer or computer terminal at the same time.

2. COPYRIGHT. The SOFTWARE is owned by Microsoft or its suppliers and is protected by United States copyright laws and international treaty provisions. Therefore, you must treat the SOFTWARE like any other copyrighted material (e.g., a book or musical recording) except that you may either (a) make one copy of the SOFTWARE solely for backup or archival purposes, or (b) transfer the SOFTWARE to a single hard disk provided you keep the original solely for backup or archival purposes. You may not copy the written materials accompanying the SOFTWARE.

3. OTHER RESTRICTIONS. You may not rent or lease the SOFTWARE, but you may transfer the SOFTWARE and accompanying written materials on a permanent basis provided you retain no copies and the recipient agrees to the terms of this Agreement. You may not reverse engineer, decompile, or disassemble the SOFTWARE. If the SOFTWARE is an update or has been updated, any transfer must include the most recent update and all prior versions.

4. DUAL MEDIA SOFTWARE. If the SOFTWARE package contains more than one kind of disk (3.5", 5.25", and CD-ROM), then you may use only the disks appropriate for your single-user computer. You may not use the other disks on another computer or loan, rent, lease, or transfer them to another user except as part of the permanent transfer (as provided above) of all SOFTWARE and written materials.

5. SAMPLE CODE. If the SOFTWARE includes Sample Code, then Microsoft grants you a royalty-free right to reproduce and distribute the sample code of the SOFTWARE provided that you: (a) distribute the sample code only in conjunction with and as a part of your software product; (b) do not use Microsoft's or its authors' names, logos, or trademarks to market your software product; (c) include the copyright notice that appears on the SOFTWARE on your product label and as a part of the sign-on message for your software product; and (d) agree to indemnify, hold harmless, and defend Microsoft and its authors from and against any claims or lawsuits, including attorneys' fees, that arise or result from the use or distribution of your software product.

DISCLAIMER OF WARRANTY

The SOFTWARE (including instructions for its use) is provided "AS IS" WITHOUT WARRANTY OF ANY KIND. MICROSOFT FURTHER DISCLAIMS ALL IMPLIED WARRANTIES INCLUDING WITHOUT LIMITATION ANY IMPLIED WARRANTIES OF MERCHANTABILITY OR OF FITNESS FOR A PARTICULAR PURPOSE. THE ENTIRE RISK ARISING OUT OF THE USE OR PERFORMANCE OF THE SOFTWARE AND DOCUMENTATION REMAINS WITH YOU.

IN NO EVENT SHALL MICROSOFT, ITS AUTHORS, OR ANYONE ELSE INVOLVED IN THE CREATION, PRODUCTION, OR DELIVERY OF THE SOFTWARE BE LIABLE FOR ANY DAMAGES WHATSOEVER (INCLUDING, WITHOUT LIMITATION, DAMAGES FOR LOSS OF BUSINESS PROFITS, BUSINESS INTERRUPTION, LOSS OF BUSINESS INFORMATION, OR OTHER PECUNIARY LOSS) ARISING OUT OF THE USE OF OR INABILITY TO USE THE SOFTWARE OR DOCUMENTATION, EVEN IF MICROSOFT HAS BEEN ADVISED OF THE POSSIBILITY OF SUCH DAMAGES. BECAUSE SOME STATES/COUNTRIES DO NOT ALLOW THE EXCLUSION OR LIMITATION OF LIABILITY FOR CONSEQUENTIAL OR INCIDENTAL DAMAGES, THE ABOVE LIMITATION MAY NOT APPLY TO YOU.

U.S. GOVERNMENT RESTRICTED RIGHTS

The SOFTWARE and documentation are provided with RESTRICTED RIGHTS. Use, duplication, or disclosure by the Government is subject to restrictions as set forth in subparagraph (c)(1)(ii) of The Rights in Technical Data and Computer Software clause at DFARS 252.227-7013 or subparagraphs (c)(1) and (2) of the Commercial Computer Software — Restricted Rights 48 CFR 52.227-19, as applicable. Manufacturer is Microsoft Corporation, One Microsoft Way, Redmond, WA 98052-6399.

If you acquired this product in the United States, this Agreement is governed by the laws of the State of Washington.

Should you have any questions concerning this Agreement, or if you desire to contact Microsoft Press for any reason, please write:

Microsoft Press, One Microsoft Way, Redmond, WA 98052-6399.

097-000-681

The
Microsoft®
Internet Explorer
Step by Step CD-ROM

The enclosed CD-ROM contains Internet Explorer 3.0; timesaving, ready-to-use practice files that complement the lessons in this book; and much more. To use the CD, you'll need the Windows 95 or Windows NT version 4.0 operating system.

Before you begin the *Step by Step* lessons, read the "Using the Microsoft Internet Explorer 3.0 Step by Step CD-ROM" section of this book. There you'll find detailed information about the contents of the CD and easy instructions telling how to install the files on your computer's hard disk.

Please take a few moments to read the License Agreement on the previous page before using the enclosed CD.

Register your Microsoft Press® book today, and let us know what you think.

At Microsoft Press, we listen to our customers. We update our books as new releases of software are issued, and we'd like you to tell us the kinds of additional information you'd find most useful in these updates. Your feedback will be considered when we prepare a future edition; plus, when you become a registered owner, you will get Microsoft Press catalogs and exclusive offers on specially priced books.

Thanks!

I used this book as

- ● A way to learn the software
- ● A reference when I needed it
- ● A way to find out about advanced features
- ● Other_____

I consider myself

- ● A beginner or an occasional computer user
- ● An intermediate-level user with a pretty good grasp of the basics
- ● An advanced user who helps and provides solutions for others
- ● Other_____

I purchased this book from

- ● A bookstore
- ● A software store
- ● A direct mail offer
- ● Other_____

I will buy the next edition of the book when it's updated

- ● Definitely
- ● Probably
- ● I will not buy the next edition

The next edition of this book should include the following additional information:

1•_____

2•_____

3•_____

The most useful things about this book are_____

_____

This book would be more helpful if_____

_____

My general impressions of this book are_____

_____

May we contact you regarding your comments?   ● Yes   ● No

Would you like to receive Microsoft Press catalogs regularly?   ● Yes   ● No

Name_____

Company (if applicable)_____

Address_____

City_____State_____Zip_____

Daytime phone number (optional) (_____)_____

Please mail back your feedback form—postage free! Fold this form as described on the other side of this card, or fax this sheet to:
Microsoft Press, Attn: Marketing Department, fax 206-936-7329

NO POSTAGE
NECESSARY
IF MAILED
IN THE
UNITED STATES

BUSINESS REPLY MAIL
FIRST-CLASS MAIL   PERMIT NO. 108   REDMOND, WA

POSTAGE WILL BE PAID BY ADDRESSEE

MICROSOFT PRESS
ONE MICROSOFT WAY
REDMOND WA 98052-9953

FOLD HERE